THIS THOUGHT'S ON ME

THIS THOUGHT'S ON ME

A Boston Guy Reflects on Leaving the Hub, Becoming a Dub & Other Topics

STEVE CORONELLA

iUniverse, Inc.
New York   Bloomington

iUniverse books may be ordered through booksellers or by contacting:

iUniverse
1663 Liberty Drive
Bloomington, IN 47403
www.iuniverse.com
1-800-Authors (1-800-288-4677)

Because of the dynamic nature of the Internet, any Web addresses or links
contained in this book may have changed since publication and may no longer be
valid. The views expressed in this work are solely those of the author and do not
necessarily reflect the views of the publisher, and the publisher hereby disclaims
any responsibility for them.

ISBN: 978-1-4401-6900-7 (sc)
ISBN: 978-1-4401-6899-4 (ebook)

Printed in the United States of America

iUniverse rev. date: 10/13/2009

To my Parents,
Phil and Phyllis Coronella
With Love

Contents

~~~~~~~

Then And Now

Out For A Laugh

Introduction: *"You Can Take The Boy Out Of Boston ..."*

IT'S ALL DOWN TO MY MOTHER, REALLY.

Back in August, 2004, I'd just returned home to Ireland after a two-week visit to Boston and Cape Cod with my wife and young son.

We'd had a great time - as we always do - connecting again with my own family and friends as well as my wife's brother and sister, who reside, handily enough, with their own families in the Framingham area.

A few days before our departure, I was leafing through my hometown paper, the *Medford Transcript*, curious to see if any names or faces from my past might pop up in the Features section or, more interestingly, the arrest reports. My mother is a dedicated subscriber to the *Transcript* - it arrives nestled in her mailbox every Thursday, notwithstanding some natural calamity - and I find it more informative than brasher papers like the *Globe* or *Herald* when it comes to keeping up with the latest news regarding my one and only hometown. (Also, very conveniently for me, it's available on-line.)

Anyway, in the course of perusing the latest edition of the *Transcript*, as well as one or two back issues, I noticed that the editor, Nell Escobar-Coakley, had foolishly issued an open appeal to her readers, inviting them (meaning me) to submit an opinion piece on any topic if sufficiently agitated to do so. Nell also included her direct e-mail address - another ill-advised move.

Well, that was enough for me. A couple of weeks later back in Dublin, I put together a compelling sales pitch for a column idea I had, entitled "At Home Abroad". (Snappy, isn't it? The alternative was "Around The World In 800 Words".) I showed the pitch to my wife - who said she was fooled, anyway - and then sent it sailing off into cyberspace, hoping it might eventually touch down near enough to Nell's e-mail inbox at the *Transcript* to draw some attention.

Happily enough, Nell was back to me in a flash. She said that a transplanted local guy's take on life abroad, mingled with memories of his Medford and Boston upbringing, sounded like a great idea. She'd be delighted to oblige.

I jumped at the opportunity. Nell even suggested that I send along a photo to accompany the column. (Presumably so that if my words failed to amuse, my picture would do the job.)

Without a hint of fanfare, then, the first installment of "At Home Abroad" appeared in September, 2004. Many more have followed since, and because my e-mail address appears at the end of each column I've been able to re-connect with old high school chums and hear from new-found readers as well. The column has also proved to be an inspiration of sorts for the freelance work I do for other Boston papers, and it has provided me with a welcome forum to sound off about the pros and cons of my new life in Ireland, using my hometown upbringing as an interesting counterpoint.

Indeed, I think Tip O'Neill would've agreed that, like politics, the best column-writing is often locally-based as well, springing from heart and home.

* * * * * * * * * *

Of course, my ultimate hope is that these essays and stories, written over the last few years, will both amuse and inform my readers, wherever you might be from. These are interesting times for an American to be living abroad. And while Dublin isn't exactly Timbuktu, it isn't Boston or Chicago or LA, either.

Ireland is a country influenced by all those places, to be sure, but it is also linked in many ways to Australia and Africa, Central America and the Far East. And as the phenomenal success of the Celtic Tiger economy attracted worldwide attention in recent years, Ireland found herself in the unlikely position of relying on immigrant labor to keep the place up and running. In a kind of bizarre role reversal, a society that regularly discarded its own people was taking in other countries' cast-offs and fortune-seekers.

The situation is, of course, very different now - given the inevitable and quite sudden downturn - and it will be fascinating to see whether Ireland will become home to those hardy souls from foreign lands who choose to stay, or whether a potentially unpleasant insularity will prevail.

As I say, interesting times indeed.

Throw in all the political and social implications of Ireland's membership in the European Union – a 27-country, nearly 500-million strong collective at last count – as well as the renewed rivalry between Europe and the US in recent years, and things get even more intriguing from an Irish-American perspective. Especially when you consider that many Yanks (and indeed even many Boston Irish) still see the Old Sod in 1950s Technicolor tones, and have yet to grasp that modernity - in all its weird and wonderful manifestations - has at last alighted on Irish shores.

So to repeat: what better time for an American with an Irish - and Italian - background to be living abroad in a country on the brink of a truly new era, which also has strong historical links to Boston.

* * * * * * * * * *

But I'm no expert commentator with a fancy degree or a make-believe title after my name. I'm just an ordinary guy with an interest in the world around him. And I'm confident these essays and stories won't let you down. (Which is more than anyone can say about the global economy at the moment.) Most of them were written during happier times, both in Ireland and the US, so if they appear on occasion to reflect a bygone era, maybe that's not such a bad thing.

Also, for the sake of coherence and readability, I've attempted to group these pieces by theme, rather than by date. As a result, my son might not appear to age progressively, as every other child does. For instance, he might be nine-years-old in one piece, only to pop up 20 pages later having regressed, Benjamin Button-like, to five or six. I'm making an authorial assumption here that my readers are clever enough to understand that the power of reverse chronology has not yet been achieved in our Dublin household.

In closing, I'd like to say thanks again to Nell Escobar-Coakley for getting the ball rolling by agreeing to run "At Home Abroad". Although not all these essays appeared originally in the *Medford Transcript* - several ran in the *Boston Globe* and *Christian Science Monitor*, many more in the *Cape Cod Times*, and a handful in the *Irish Times* - it was her commitment to my idea that suggested the basis for this book.

(Bill O'Neill, formerly of the *Cape Cod Times*, also deserves an exceedingly honorable mention here. I used my six years living on the Cape as material for several pieces, and Bill's eager acceptance of my work was a great encouragement. Kim Tan at the *Globe* also gave me the space and support to develop my ideas, and I'm grateful to him for that. At the *Monitor*, Clara Germani, Kendra Nordin, and Judy Lowe offered some very helpful advice - my thanks to them all - and through the *Monitor*'s syndication service my work got a wider distribution, appearing in newspapers in Alaska, California, Texas, and the American South.)

As for the funny stuff featured in the final section, "Out for a Laugh", my inspiration there can be traced to a long line of eminent American humorists, from S.J. Perelman and James Thurber, to Garrison Keillor and Dave Barry, to name but a few. Each of them, to a man, shares in whatever credit is due these stories. (And they remain blameless for any shortcomings.)

But the ultimate expression of gratitude goes, as always, to my mother, Phyllis Coronella - who has legitimate up-to-date links to Cork, by the way - for her continuing support over the years. And for getting the hometown paper every week and sharing it with me.

- Dublin, Ireland and Medford, Massachusetts
March, 2009

At Home Abroad

An Accidental Irishman

~~~~~~~~~~

COME THE FIRST OF SEPTEMBER my son begins school here in Dublin, and though he's had all the right credentials for some time now, I suppose this marks his official arrival as an Irish citizen.

He's perfectly fine with this turn of events, excited even, but it's got me to thinking about identity and belonging, as defined by birthright and nationality. Sounds very high-minded and abstract, I know, but I'm useless at the really important things such as arranging all the necessary paperwork and organizing a set of clothes for the occasion. My wife is far handier there.

So I'm left to do the dreamier stuff. I've been meditating on how the chance circumstances of a child's birth - where he's delivered into this world, and who his parents are - can determine the course of a young life before it has barely begun.

My relocation to Ireland in 1992 was a considered move, but also unexpected in its way. Back in the 1980s, I'd entertained romantic notions of moving here for a while, especially after several tours of the island (in the company of friends and on my own), and I kept up contact with my grandmother's family in Cork, just in case.

In truth, though, it was all a youthful fancy. After graduating from college, I settled on Cape Cod. Real life intervened: a car, a job, a succession of roofs over my head. Then, within a period of 18 months, I was introduced to my future wife, traded letters and visits with her across the water, moved to Dublin, and was married. Never in that time did I give serious consideration to the implications of bringing up a child outside the land of my own birth. As my wife will confirm, I don't plan that far ahead for anything.

But now one of life's watershed moments draws near. As my son's first day of school approaches, I've come to grasp that Brian will be embarking on a journey that I have not undertaken myself: the system, the setting that he's about to enter is as new to me as it is to him. So, as regards his schooling anyway, he'll be guiding me as much as I'll be guiding him. Which is just another interesting offshoot of my son's status as an "accidental Irishman".

It's also occurring to me that the true comforts of home, so to speak, are often intangible and exist in the realm of the imagination. According to the Central Statistics Office in Dublin, since the Celtic Tiger economy hit stride in 1996, 45% of immigrants into Ireland have been the Irish themselves, returning from often successful lives abroad. Many of these are Irish couples who decided to come home from the States when their kids reached school-going age. I can now understand their point.

As I see it, they're hesitant – maybe even a little fearful – about sending their kids through a system they haven't experienced themselves. Sure, math is math, English is English, wherever these subjects are taught in the world, and these returning Irish parents know that. Also, in many cases, the resources and opportunities for their kids would be better in the States. But what brings them back home, I'm convinced, is their unshakeable belief that the US system is beyond their understanding (and thus, in their minds, inferior) because they haven't gone through it themselves. I find myself questioning the Irish educational system for precisely the same reason.

And like ex-pat parents everywhere, I know that there are other limits I'll encounter.

Each of us possesses a profound geography of memory that only our homeplace can evoke, and it is dawning on me now, as my son becomes a boy (and then a man), that I'll never be able to pass a ball field with him in Dublin and say: *See that park, that's where your grandfather taught me how to hit a baseball.* Or tell him: *Down along the river there, that's where your uncle and I used to spend hours fishing.*

Both my wife and I are relative newcomers to the small town ten miles south of Dublin that we now call home, so it'll be our son Brian who will put the more lasting family stamp on the place, and create the most memories here.

And that's where my own family history comes full circle, I suppose. My maternal grandparents left Cork around 1930, to settle in Cambridge, and now I've returned to Ireland to relive their experience in reverse. Minus the hardship and deprivation and heartbreaking separation from family that they went through, needless to say. Like them, I've set up home and established a family in a land that will never have the same pull on my emotions and imagination as my birthplace.

Curiously enough, though, raising a child abroad has made me keenly aware of my own deeply-sown roots back home in Medford, Massachusetts – even more so than if I'd never moved away.

Which brings us back to Brian, and the opportunities that lie ahead of him owing to the chance circumstances of his birth. In time to come, maybe all my twittering-on about family and remembrance will mean something to him. Maybe not. But whatever the outcome of his life – should he end up back in Boston or decide to stay in Dublin – he'll always be able to say that if nothing else, his journey was an interesting one.

Right Wing, Wrong Man
For Irish Airwaves

As a stay-at-home suburban dad, I encounter few enough opportunities, on a daily basis, for international celebrity. But thanks to President Bush and his neo-con cronies, who've decided that conquering Iraq constitutes a first tentative step towards world peace, I very nearly became the Rush Limbaugh of Ireland.

Here's how my meteoric rise as a media superstar almost happened in the days leading up to the US takedown of Saddam Hussein:

Having dropped my son to pre-school, I was sitting at home in front of my computer, fiddling innocently with some correspondence. The radio played in the background. To my surprise, an offhand quip I'd dispatched via e-mail to a popular current affairs program was read over the air. *Steve Coronella from Shankill writes to say ...* That kind of thing. I gave in to a self-satisfied little smile. You see, I spend a lot of time at home, looking after my young son while trying to write the Next Big Book to come out of Ireland. Sending up flares like this every now and again helps to keep me in touch with the outside world.

A short time later, though, the plot thickened. On the way to collect my son, I stopped by a local convenience store to buy the *Irish Times*. On the editorial page was a letter I'd written, which criticized the peculiar brand of neutrality practiced in Ireland. In the letter I identified myself as an American who held dual citizenship. This, I felt, allowed me to comment on the domestic policies of my adopted home. Again, I allowed myself a small degree of satisfaction that my thoughts were deemed worthy for general distribution.

I brought my son home, we had lunch, and then I remembered to check for any phone messages. There was indeed one, from the producer of a Sunday night TV discussion program. She'd read my letter in the *Irish Times*, and was wondering if I might ring her back for a brief chat. Indeed. Another of my little flares had not only drawn some attention, it had been traced back to me.

With my son settled quietly in front of a video (President Bush would be delighted to learn that he's into *Justice League* at the moment), I phoned Roisin Boyd in her office at RTE, Ireland's national broadcaster. Ms. Boyd thanked me for returning her call and mentioned my letter again. Then she got down to business. Did I consider the protests taking place over US troops using Shannon Airport on their way to the Gulf anti-American? she asked. And was I pro-war?

As I say, in my letter I criticized Irish neutrality, basically pointing out that given Ireland's extremely vulnerable defense forces and the country's overall dependence on the US and Britain, genuine neutrality is a luxury that the Irish state simply cannot afford.

Having dismissed the self-righteous fence-straddling of the Irish government - which has pretty much turned a blind eye to the US military's use of a quiet airport on the west coast here - how did I respond to Ms. Boyd's queries about my own political inclinations? Well, I attempted a careful balancing act of my own.

It would be hard not to see the protests as anti-American, I said. (The feeling you get sometimes from peace activists such as those shouting their mindless slogans outside Shannon Airport is that the world would be a better place if not a single US soldier - or US tourist for that matter - strayed out of their national territory.)

On the other hand, I added, I wasn't convinced that a pre-emptive war was the best way to deal with Saddam. I then went on to express my general unease about our President, noting in particular his Road to Damascus-type conversion, post 9/11, in respect to US commitments and initiatives abroad.

I could sense in Ms. Boyd's polite acknowledgements that I wasn't nearly combative enough to make for good television, and indeed the offer of a place on her panel of pundits never came. "We're having no trouble finding people who are anti-war," she said. "It's finding people who are in favor of it that's the problem."

In the end I never got my quarter hour of fame - or infamy, more precisely, given the hostility expressed on Irish TV and radio to official US policy concerning Iraq.

So Rush, old boy, your job remains safe for now. But the next time an unpopular cause (preferably right-wing and Republican) needs an advocate in Ireland, I'm taking the job.

A Homecoming In Sicily

WHEN I FIRST MOVED TO IRELAND, MY surname presented certain problems. From the start, Irish people jokingly called me Steve "Cornetto", after a popular ice cream treat. Then there were the obvious gibes inspired by films such as *The Godfather* and *Goodfellas*. Even though they couldn't pronounce it, everyone assumed from my last name that I knew the likes of Tony Soprano personally. At other times, ignoring any possible connections I might have in the worlds of *haute couture* or top-level European soccer, people might ask if I was friendly with the family that runs our local chipper. (The clue here is that Dublin's best-known fish and chip shops happen to be operated by folks of Italian origin.)

So you can see that during my early years in Ireland I had to grin and bear the sort of stupid stereotyping that the Irish themselves have endured for centuries.

Go figure.

Of course, anyone who was genuinely curious about my surname got a more agreeable reaction. After making sure there wasn't a stereotype in sight, I'd relate the following tale.

* * * * * * * * * *

In the spring of 1986, after several weeks of trains, planes, and the occasional automobile, I found myself sitting alone on an unfamiliar doorstep in Sicily. I also found myself questioning the wisdom of traveling 5,000 miles from my family home in Medford to revive my father's neglected lineage.

In the six-unit apartment block behind me lived my father's uncle Francesco. We had never met. In fact, I wondered if he knew I existed at all.

From wary neighbors I learned that Uncle Francesco and his family would be returning home in about an hour, for their midday meal. One hour stretched uncomfortably into two. My doubts grew. Why was I here? What did I hope to discover?

My adventure was part genealogical dig, part self-exploration. After my third visit to Ireland in the 1980s, I'd become our family's informal historian, examining photo albums and home movies with a fresh eye, listening patiently and carefully to my grandmother's surprisingly clear-eyed memories of her younger days in Cork. She had emigrated in 1930 and settled with my grandfather on Tierney Street in Cambridge.

Yet my father's family remained a mystery. His parents continued to speak Italian throughout the four decades they lived in Boston's West End neighborhood and then in South Medford, only occasionally admitting a colloquial phrase or a few words of English into their conversation. This proved to be an impassable barrier to any meaningful exchanges between us, and they died in the early 1970s, before my curiosity and interest in them was awakened.

As a result, I knew little of their lives. I was in Augusta, Sicily, to collect any clues that might help me understand them better.

Uncle Francesco, his wife, Maria, and son, Cesare, finally arrived home. By a process of elimination - all the other residents of the apartment block had passed me already - I was fairly certain of their identity. They got out of their car and approached the front door.

"Signor Rizza?" I asked.

"*Sì.*"

"*Mi chiamo* Stephen Coronella. *Nonna mia* ..." My fund of Italian phrases was spent after two sentences. I resumed my explanation in rapid-delivery English. "My grandmother was your sister, which means that my father ..."

Cesare waved my verbal express to a halt while directing me upstairs to the family's apartment. "Too much, too much," he said with a shrug and a smile.

Once inside, Cesare disappeared for a moment and came back carrying an enormous blue book with a battered front cover. It was an Italian-English dictionary that both of us could use. The book had been collecting dust for almost 10 years, ever since Cesare completed his last university course in English.

We spent the afternoon pushing it at one another across the table in the TV room. Just as soon as we had cleared one linguistic hurdle, another popped up, and it was back to the book.

But Cesare could not always be around to act as interpreter, and it was during these absences that I grew closer to Uncle Francesco. My visit stirred something in him. Perhaps I was a living testament to his departed sister's life in America, a life he had only glimpsed through occasional letters and infrequent photographs.

One afternoon we went visiting together - my sudden appearance had generated much curiosity - and afterward strolled the streets of Augusta, with Uncle Francesco acting as tour guide.

Using a sparse medley of English, French, and Italian phrases, I asked Uncle Francesco to show me where my grandparents had lived before they sailed for Boston. We made an unlikely couple, the old retired gentleman dressed impeccably in coat and tie, careful to doff his hat to passing ladies, and the curious traveler in fading, weathered jeans and unfashionable hiking boots.

We found the building my grandparents had once called home, and we paused for a moment. But in the bustle of late afternoon, it was hard to imagine the same scene as it might have appeared 60 years before to a couple of Boston-bound newlyweds.

Farther along, we stopped in front of a sporting goods store. By placing his hands together, then resting his head sideways upon them and bawling quietly like a baby, Uncle Francesco indicated that this was his birthplace, there in the back, where now they restring tennis rackets. The memory, and his own ridiculous pantomime, made him laugh softly to himself.

Back at home, we looked over his stamp and coin collections, finding that we needed the big blue book less and less to communicate. Or so it seemed. As a memento of my visit, Uncle Francesco gave me a rare 500-lire coin, along with a meticulous copy of our family tree, hand-drawn on white typewriter paper. In the lower right corner he wrote a simple message to my father, Phil, a sort of gentle study guide: *Remember PHILIP, Uncle Francesco*. I was leaving the next day.

On the way to the train station, Cesare explained that my visit was important to his father, and it was important, too, that we stay in touch.

It was raining over Sicily the night I returned to Rome, though I hardly noticed. Thanks to an old man's soft-spoken joy, a light shone where none had shone before. As it turned out, lugging a 40-pound backpack all the way from Boston, then across Ireland, England, and France, before finally "coming home" in Sicily, had been well worth the effort.

And that's why, as I continue to explain to my Irish friends, the name is Coronella.

An Irish Road Worrier
Dishes The Dirt

~~~~~~~~~

IF YOU WEREN'T ABLE TO make it to Ireland for St. Patrick's Day, chances are you're planning a summer visit.

Since moving here from Boston nearly twenty years ago, I've negotiated roads of every description in Dublin and beyond. And I'm here to offer a bit of advice on a subject that the guidebooks generally ignore: driving your rental car around Ireland.

Of course, if gaping potholes, unmarked detours, and an absence of any kind of road authority are your thing - and why shouldn't they be after two decades of the Big Dig - then there's nothing to worry about. But just in case, here's a brief motoring guide to bring you up to speed, as it were, with the driving conditions you're likely to find on the Emerald Isle.

Speed Limits

To put it mildly, the Irish police force, or Garda Siochana, is having trouble keeping up with the society it's been assigned to protect. Top-of-the-line Saabs, Volvos, BMWs and Mercedes regularly crowd the roads, while Irish cops continue to putter around in battered midsize sedans streaked with grime and often missing their hubcaps.

In other words, though you might encounter the occasional speed gun-wielding Irish cop on a straight stretch of the newer roads here, the Force definitely won't be there to guide and protect you on the more perilous secondary routes.

For instance, as you drive around Ireland, especially "down the country", you'll encounter fellow motorists who appear to be auditioning for next year's Indy 500. They'll zoom up to your rear bumper, materializing out of nowhere, and then, spotting an inch of space, dart around you and take off for the horizon. Under ideal conditions, there'd be an officer over the next hill to nab these hot-rodders. But no, there's not a squad car in sight, just a herd of bemused cows wondering at all the commotion.

To offset these maniacal "road users", however, there are Ireland's ploughboys - and I mean that literally. A lone tractor will often be at the head of a winding, slow-moving column of traffic that only clears when the blockading farmer elects to pull over, or when he realizes that he's overshot his own field by a mile and a half.

As you drive through towns and villages across Ireland, then, it's helpful to remember that an Irishman in control of a commercial vehicle is an obstruction waiting to happen.

So my general advice here is: *semper paratus*.

Road Signs

Ignore Irish road signs unless you are desperate and have no other option. Often two signs for the same destination can be pointing *in opposite directions*. As a result, you could, theoretically, spend the entire two weeks of your holiday driving up and down, back and forth, along the same windswept laneway somewhere in County Clare. Of course, you can always stop to ask directions, although it must be said that this option will likely take a week off your vacation as well.

The lonesome-looking pensioner dawdling along the road, tapping his walking stick contemplatively as he goes, won't let you pass without offering you a colorful summary of his local and personal history.

This prospect shouldn't worry you, however. Depending on the quality of the encounter, the few moments you spend with this gentleman might feature later as a highlight of your visit.

Another important fact: Irish speed limits are now measured in kilometers, not miles – though the signs for such are small and round and hard to spot unless you know where to look. In this area, as in the others I've mentioned, having a competent co-pilot beside you is crucial if you want to survive your Irish driving holiday without suffering a serious neurological breakdown.

And as for planning your itinerary? Don't impose an American mindset on your travels, since distances in Ireland - which have also gone metric - can be extremely subjective. One man's "follow the road for a wee stretch as far as Egan's pub" is another's 10k. So be prepared to find yourself getting ever closer to a delightful Connemara village (described lovingly in your guidebook) that you actually drove through the day before.

My rule of thumb then: enjoy where you are, when you get there.

Driving Technique

Many Irish drivers appear to have progressed only in recent weeks from a horse and buggy to a motor car. Offensive claptrap, you say? Just wait and see for yourself. For every Indy 500 wannabe, there are just as many drivers who look decidedly ill-at-ease behind the wheel. (In fact, as you'll be all bleary-eyed and disheveled after your overnight flight from the States, this could be you.)

Hands clenched to the wheel, eyes locked forward, these people putter along with an amazing disregard for the world beyond their windshield. Unfortunately, on long stretches of road in Ireland, there can be little opportunity to "overtake" such drivers. So, after you've been on their tail for 20 or 30 minutes, you begin to study them, and get inside their head, and pretty soon, you too will become apprehensive about driving any faster than 50 kilometers per hour.

(Of course, most rental cars in Ireland are standard shift, so you might not be able to get out of second gear anyway.)

Bottom line, though: going native in this regard will win you no friends.

Parking

One final word about dropping your car when you get where you're going. Parking a car can be a hit (quite literally) or miss proposition with many Irish drivers.

Even though most parking lots (or car parks) have clearly identifiable white lines, to mark out individual spaces, this means nothing. The Irish spirit, so amenable to contrariness in all its forms, can often be seen at work in public parking spaces. Zig-zag, askew, butt-end out into approaching traffic - this is how the Irish prefer to leave their resting vehicles.

Your rental company, I'm sure, though, will want you to follow accepted international practice here. Park your car carefully, between white lines where provided (and when you can fit), and pay whatever tariff is asked of you.

This will prove very un-Irish, but since you've been spotted on the road already, respecting the speed limit while at the same time looking out for any helpful signs or watchful police, well, the jig's been up for a while, my friend.

From 9 To 5, A Good Man
Is Hard To Find

~~~~~~~~~

EVERY NEIGHBORHOOD, INDEED EVERY COMMUNITY, could use
a few good men like me.

Before you dismiss me as a self-regarding promoter of non-
PC gender issues - now there's a mouthful - hear me out.

I work at home, combining the full-time care of my young
son with the punishing task of getting my first novel into the
hands of a sympathetic publisher. (Freelance efforts such at this
I regard as a necessary therapy.)

But I'm also available for the odd bit of grass-cutting and
minor household maintenance for an older neighbor, and
a short while back I helped out at my son's school when the
custodian there suddenly resigned.

My mere presence at home during the day can be just
as valuable, and not simply where my son is concerned. The
residents of our quiet suburban street benefit as well. House
break-ins are common enough in Dublin, no matter where you
live, and I like to think of myself as the best burglar repellent
on the market.

As I say, this is no cheap promotional stunt on my part.

Rather, I'm trying to make an important point. Far from being professional failures or general ne'er-do-wells, men who aren't formally employed can contribute significantly to the welfare and smooth running of a community, either on a one-to-one basis (as with a neighbor) or where a local agency (such as a school) is concerned.

I can still feel a little awkward, almost embarrassed, when new acquaintances here inquire about my occupation. Because I'm an American residing in Ireland, people feel safe enough following this line. After all, no one decides to live abroad without first lining up a job. But when I offer my reply - *I'm at home minding my son and doing some writing* - it soon becomes clear this is not the expected answer. The questions people then want to ask remain largely unspoken, but I still hear them. *What do I do with myself all day (especially before Brian came along)? And with my wife out at work and no family in the area, am I not driven mad by the isolation (even after Brian arrived)?*

After a few uncomfortable moments we usually move on to safer topics, like politics and religion, but I can't help feeling that such exchanges somehow diminish me in other people's estimation.

Even in this enlightened age, a stay-at-home dad is a rarity. Despite what the feature pages have to say, it's still a woman's world, in a domestic sense, from nine to five, Monday to Friday. Here in Ireland, the figures definitely bear this out. In the 2002 census, more than 21,000 men listed their primary occupation as looking after their home and family (up from a meager 4,138 in 1996). But that number compares poorly to the nearly 418,000 women working in the home (down from 549,000 in 1996).

Given this numerical imbalance, it's hardly surprising that at certain times of the day, we're nowhere to be found in the community.

But who exactly is responsible for this scarcity of men on the home front? Well, we men are – at least partly. Being a full-time father to one's kids and the co-manager of a household doesn't seem to amount to much in the greater scheme of things. Most men need outside validation, the kind of imprimatur provided by a successful business venture or a triumphant sporting achievement. And, I have to confess, that was once a big stumbling block for me. My roles in life, I've come to conclude, are two-fold: father and writer, with the scrivener's trade taking a back seat to my paternal calling, for the moment anyway.

Does it appear that I'm overselling myself? No, I don't think so. When men become available for family and community service during hours in which they are otherwise missing in action, then everyone wins, from the kids at home, to the neighbor next door, to the school or library program that needs a helping hand.

So men, don't give up hope just yet. Even if we are eventually engineered out of the reproductive process, there'll still be room for us in other areas of communal life.

But I wouldn't wait too long to inquire about any vacancies.

Forget Top Billing When You're A Sidekick Dad

MAYBE IT'S BECAUSE ANOTHER FATHER'S Day is just around the corner, but I'm finally starting to make sense of the particular frustrations that come with being a stay-at-home dad.

So what's my big discovery concerning fatherhood? Well, it's simple really. With the arrival of my son eight years ago this month, I went from being a headline act to a sidekick overnight.

(When I help out on school trips, for instance, I have a fulfilling, though relatively minor role as "Brian's dad".)

From this eureka moment has come a further set of insights.

I now understand why so many men are reluctant to take up the full-time care of their children. A parent's work, by and large, is unproductive. (In the traditional free market economy sense, that is.) We spend a good deal of time shifting uncomfortably on the sidelines, as our kids go from one activity to another or simply hang out around the house with their friends. For our efforts, the most we can hope for at the end of each day is to see a happy and untroubled child, resting peaceably.

This is a concept alien to a lot of men, myself included. Due to my hard-wiring (or maybe hard-headedness), I often get the feeling that I should be doing something more substantial and, yes, more productive with my time. Looking after my son, preparing the evening meal, and sorting through laundry while my wife is at work - these hardly seem the tasks of a "real man."

Part of this is society's fault, of course. (And no better culprit.) Here in Ireland, for instance, stay-at-home dads are a decided minority: 21,000 of us compared to nearly 418,000 housekeeping moms. (I'm sure the same ratio applies around Boston.)

It's a hard sell, whichever way you look at it. Most people, if they allowed their prejudices full expression, would probably say that full-time dads fall into two categories: lay-abouts or wusses. Neither of which looks good on a résumé.

And yet, wouldn't most kids jump at the chance to have their dad around all day? The trouble with that setup, of course, is that boys will be boys. Speaking from experience, I find that it's difficult not to revert to the carefree ease of childhood when tedious household chores beckon. Whether I'm out kicking a soccer ball with my son or walking behind him as he rollerblades around our suburban Dublin neighborhood, I have no trouble imagining that I'm eight-years-old again myself. (My wife will back me on this one, and she might even lower that age threshold a bit.)

Of course, no matter who's minding the kids, one thing is for sure: well-adjusted children don't spring up overnight. And this is where men (and some women) need to broaden their understanding of what goes on after they leave the house for work each day. Mothers and fathers who stay at home with their kids have to be as innovative and resourceful as any business executive. But where parenting is concerned, there is seldom a visible payoff. Or more precisely, the payoffs that do occur, in the form of a sheltering home space distinguished by a reliable laundry service and a well-stocked fridge, are often taken for granted.

Of course, I've hardly touched on an equally vexing problem.

Due to economic pressures, most couples can't even contemplate the option of one parent staying at home with the kids. When I was a Medford youth of impressionable age - back in the late 1960s, early 1970s, if you're curious - there was always someone, most certainly a mom, tending the home front. And such were the times that we even walked home from school for our lunch, then trudged back for another couple of hours of instruction in the afternoon. Ah, the innocence of it all.

That would be impossible today. In most households now, both parents are working, to support the mortgage, the cars, and the gadgets. Even if dear old dad wanted to stay at home and play straight man to his kids, the numbers simply wouldn't add up at the end of each month.

So I suppose it doesn't really matter whether being a stay-at-home dad has reduced me to a lowly sidekick. I should count myself lucky this Father's Day that I'm on the bill at all.

One-Size Yuletide
Not Always A Good Fit

~~~~~~~~~~

I'VE BEEN LIVING IN IRELAND for nearly two decades now. During that time the country has changed beyond recognition. And that's become a problem not just for tourists - who expect to see the country their parents or grandparents left behind - but for some native Irish people as well.

The trouble, as they see it, is that Ireland is losing its cultural identity under an onslaught of foreign influences. In particular, they worry that folks here are morphing into clone-like duplicates of their US cousins.

Take my word: there's a wide gulf yet between the two countries. But I will concede that the Irish have embraced the American way when it comes to celebrating certain holidays.

The Fourth of July, for instance, gets pretty good recognition here, and Halloween has taken on American trappings, with house decorations, store-bought costumes, and trick-or-treating on an entrepreneurial level now featuring prominently.

But at no time of the year is the "Americanization" of Irish customs more evident than at Christmas. The consumer aspect has come to dominate the holiday here as well. Vast new shopping malls have sprung up around the country in recent years, and the Irish response has been no different from that of people everywhere: build them and we will come.

Certainly, small town Irish merchants in the past were dependent on a busy and lucrative Yuletide season to carry them through quieter periods in the year. But back then, shop owners forged personal relationships with their customers that helped sustain a viable year-round business. When we visit Bandon, my wife's hometown 20 miles west of Cork city, I can see locally-owned businesses struggling to survive as townspeople flock to the latest wonder mall, where they are just another nameless face in the crowd, looking for a bargain.

Christmas in Ireland used to be mainly a social holiday – more like Thanksgiving in the US, with the emphasis on food and companionship. Friends and relations would often return home from abroad, and then set off again a week or two later, perhaps not to be seen for another few years.

This is something I've experienced first-hand. Back in the winter of 1985-86, I visited family and friends in Cork and Dublin, and the near absence of Yuletide glitz startled me. I was also bemused that the country simply shut down over Christmas.

In those darker economic times, people fortunate enough to have a job here were employed either in the civil service or by the banks. As a result, if you needed to inquire about your financial affairs, or arrange a passport or mail a package, you were just plain out of luck. Nothing was open for nearly a fortnight.

Today, that is all changed utterly. Many American companies are now based here, and while they indulge the laid-back Irish mentality to some extent, it's back to "business as usual" as soon after Christmas as they can get away with. And because business thrives on business, a lot of Irish retailers have followed suit, and they too reopen their doors a day or so after Christmas.

As well, low-cost air travel means Irish people abroad can

come and go more frequently and at different times of the year, so a two-week nationwide work stoppage in late December is no longer necessary to welcome back these displaced sons and daughters.

As I survey the scene here in Dublin and around Boston on my own visits home, I find reasons to be both hopeful and disheartened this holiday season. On both sides of the water, I see people who have developed businesses or started up community projects in the small openings that still appear in the broader global economy. Personal initiative and sacrifice, it seems, haven't quite gone out of fashion.

But I also see people, especially here in newly-affluent Dublin, whose lives are distinguished by an unflattering superficiality. These *nouveau riche* Irish are enjoying all the status-enhancing perks of their sudden wealth without any sense – yet – of a greater civic responsibility. (Incredibly, this too is sometimes blamed on American influence.)

But this wasn't meant to be a bah-humbug piece, with the Grinch as my muse. At this time of year, I believe, communities and individuals invariably find their own ways to express a general goodwill.

And I'd like that to be my ultimate message today.

The Down-Home Appeal
Of Gaelic Games

MY EIGHT-YEAR-OLD SON has yet to declare a favorite where sports are concerned.

For the moment he follows the seasons - soccer when the English Premier League is in session, baseball as soon as Opening Day at Fenway rolls around. And he exemplifies that approach on the road outside our Dublin home. It doesn't matter whether he's kicking a ball or throwing one. As long as he's moving, that's what counts.

Two or three years down the line, though, I expect he'll look to me for some guidance. He'll want me to nudge him toward a preferred game, all the while hoping that his dad is still sound enough of mind and body to avoid embarrassing him on - and off - the playing field.

But given that baseball is still very much an up-and-coming game here and public basketball and tennis courts a rarity, what exactly are my options as far as youth sports programs are concerned?

Well, in Ireland, as in the rest of Europe, soccer is the dominant game. Italy, Spain, Germany, and England are home to the finest domestic leagues in the world, drawing players from all corners of the globe. The intensive marketing of this sports product is aimed at kids and adults alike, as the recent mega-signing of David Beckham by the LA Galaxy shows.

This presents me (and my son) with two problems. First, I don't have the makings of a proper Soccer Dad. My feet were made for walking, on a good day, not for the kind of nimble pirouettes I see kids performing at my son's weekend league games. So when Brian comes up to me, as he already has, looking for some basic pointers in the game, let's just say he might as well ask me to teach him to dance like Gene Kelly.

Second, an early preference for soccer will prove costly before too long. In fact, my wife and I are already under pressure to buy any knick-knack or article of clothing that bears a cherished team logo (which, given historical precedent and marketing savvy, will most likely belong to Manchester United). These must-have items are sold at outrageously-inflated prices to bolster the coffers of teams that most kids will never see play in person. This gear also possesses a kind of street cred that I have trouble fathoming, which encourages kids to root only for successful teams.

With these misgivings in mind, where does a parent like me turn? In my own formative years, back in Boston, we had Bobby Orr and The Big, Bad Bruins, while over at Fenway, Yaz and Rico were performing improbable deeds.

Here in Ireland there is the GAA, or Gaelic Athletic Association.

Imagine an organization and a set of games with the historical pull of baseball, the frenetic energy of playoff hockey, and the broad presence of high school football.

That would be the GAA in Ireland.

Established in 1884 in a Tipperary hotel as a means of preserving Ireland's national identity through her native games, the GAA still enjoys a grass-roots appeal that other sports organizations can only dream of.

In his book, *Green Fields - Gaelic Sport in Ireland*, sportswriter Tom Humphries offers a possible explanation: "Today, three-quarters of a million Irish people are members of the GAA, but this figure represents only a fraction of the Irish people who are touched by the games of football and hurling in their daily lives. The influence of the GAA cannot be measured in units of membership or revenue, through attendance or viewing figures. Its impact is emotional, visceral."

The GAA is also distinctive in a way that any parent can appreciate.

We tend to cast prominent athletes as role model for our kids. And then we curse these demi-gods when they are shown to be altogether human - only more so, given the amazing riches at their disposal. Being community-based and amateur, the GAA has yet to run into this problem. After every match players return to the real world, where there's a daily job to be tended and a home life to be cultivated, usually not far from the place where they were reared.

The day the GAA loses this grass-roots communal bond, its mission in Irish life will have vanished.

As for my son, I'll guide him and offer advice as best I can. And should he want to try Gaelic football or hurling at some stage, I won't object, despite my own ineptitude at these games.

In a sports world gone crazy with money and celebrity, the GAA's core values of continuity and community don't look half bad.

Kneeling At The Crossroads

~~~~~~~~~

THANKS TO MY SON, I'VE reached another of life's crossroads.

As he has a habit of doing, my nine-year-old boy is forcing me to make some hard choices, most recently regarding the importance (or not) of a religious influence in his life.

Perhaps a little background would be helpful here. Like many people of my generation, I haven't been a regular church-goer for most of my adult life. I fell into that convenient category called "Lapsed Catholics".

But here in Ireland, where the Catholic Church still oversees the vast majority of primary schools, a young child's participation in First Communion festivities is pretty much a given. So, anticipating the day when my son might indeed take part himself - which he did last spring - I returned to the fold, on a semi-regular basis, a few years back.

It all sounds very calculating and cynical, I know. But deep down, something else was stirring. I could feel the old familiar ways beckoning as well.

And this is no bad thing. Without doubt the qualities promoted at Mass each week are admirable ones: decency, charity, and compassion toward one's fellows.

Steve Coronella

But some of my youthful misgivings - voiced around the family dinner table in years past - still trouble me.

Reading newspaper accounts of the latest financial or sexual abuse scandals, one might easily conclude that the Church has lost the plot over the years. When I sit with my son at Mass, listening to the Gospel and then the priest's homily, I often wonder why it's not possible to aspire toward the Christian ideal without buying into all the extraneous theological trappings, added on, in some cases, hundreds of years after the Crucifixion. Does Christ's message, as embodied in the Beatitudes, not lay out a radical enough agenda?

On a personal level, there's an even more difficult challenge. How do I reconcile my attendance at Mass with the substantial doubts I have about the foundations of my faith?

This is where our kids come into the picture. It's also where I might offer a helpful analogy. Between religion and food, no less.

My son is nine and has quite an appetite at times. I've found that giving him a menu to select from, when he's hungry, can be counter-productive. He'll hem and haw, decide and un-decide, mainly because he's starving. Better to just serve something up - ensuring that it's healthy and wholesome (for the most part) - and take my chances. More times than not, he'll eat what's on offer and be glad of it. When he's older and doesn't like my choice of grub, he can cook up something for himself.

I believe the same goes with religion. Give a child a choice of faiths (or none at all), and the result will be confusion and a continuing hunger. Better to provide a few items of substance, celestially speaking, and nourish the child on that. When he's older and finds the recipe unsatisfactory, he can put together something for himself in the way of belief systems.

That's my thinking on the subject anyway. It's a general approach that seems to be working for the moment, and I have no trouble explaining to my son concepts that clash with my own understanding of life - and death.

Take the notion of heaven, for instance, which most kids are able to tap into quite easily. Without being sarcastic or dismissive, I have gladly painted a picture of heavenly paradise for my son - even though human memory is the afterlife I believe in. This may sound arrogant or presumptuous, but I see it as a transcendent thing.

After we die, we live on (if we're lucky) in the hearts and minds of those we loved and those who loved us. We recall our moms and dads to our kids, and they remember us to their children. I can think of no more glorious or honorable an outcome to a life than this.

So am I a coward or a hypocrite, or perhaps an even more contemptible combination of the two, for not sticking to the letter of my beliefs?

Well, none of the above, actually. I believe we can be practical and transcendent at the same time, that we can celebrate human existence and all its possibilities - through art and music and literature - without compromising our visionary intelligence. And sometimes, especially when dealing with kids, this requires more than just a simple recitation of accepted dogma.

So if my son comes looking for some extra instruction, how exactly will I elaborate on the mystery of the Eucharist, which he now eagerly receives when we attend Mass? I'm still working on that one. But I do know that I'll have a ready pupil - my son is inquisitive and capable of wonder in equal measure - and I'm confident he'll come to understand how a simple Communion wafer can have a grander significance.

For the moment then, we'll continue to attend Mass as often as we can. And we'll come away, like those around us, committed to working toward a finer sense of ourselves.

No Blarney, I'm Raising A Dub!

~~~~~~~~~~

I REALIZE THAT ST PATRICK'S Day is approaching and we're all meant to be nice to the Irish. But there are two sides to every story, especially where Ireland's biggest city is concerned.

You see, throughout the rest of the country, Dublin has a bit of a reputation. (Come to think of it, even among many Dubliners, the city gets a bad rap.)

The Irish capital is seen as dirty and dangerous, growing too fast and in too many directions, creating more problems (for itself and the country generally) than it can possibly handle.

The Greater Dublin area - which, practically speaking, now takes in parts of the adjoining counties of Meath, Kildare, Louth, and Wicklow - is home to one-third of the Republic's population.

This is due to a sort of Catch-22 scenario. Because businesses clustered around the capital have ready access to large numbers of skilled workers, the Dublin region attracts by far the greatest amount of foreign investment into Ireland. To feed this growth, more and more recruits arrive from remoter parts of the country (and, increasingly, from eastern Europe), thus tilting the population imbalance even further.

As a result, so-called economic black spots around Ireland

are made even less appealing for development, owing to their neglected infrastructure and declining local communities.

And the crowning indignity: Dublin is, verifiably, one of the most expensive European cities in which to live or run a business.

So, having sketched a pretty unflattering portrait of the city I now call home, I have a confession to make. Despite the fact that my wife is from Cork and I can claim full privileges as a Boston guy and limited rights as a Cape Codder, I'm raising a Dub!

Yes, though he holds dual citizenship and spends time with his cousins around Boston each summer, my young son will, in years to come, identify Dublin as his hometown. He already roots for Dublin's Gaelic sports teams - although, through careful product placement around our house, he has a definite affection for the Cork hurling team and, of course, the Red Sox.

Without doubt, raising a child in a country or even a city that isn't your own can have subtle effects on your parenting. For instance, in the absence of any immediate family or convenient geographical prompts, a conscious effort is required to make your child aware of his roots. You'll rarely share any casual memories stirred by familiar landmarks around town, such as, in my case, the basketball court and baseball diamond at my neighborhood park in Medford, or the touched-up facade of my old elementary school, now a Tufts University administration building.

As I see it, this is perhaps the most difficult part of living abroad: conducting your day-to-day life in a landscape that holds only very recent personal memories.

Of course, living in a foreign land can have a liberating effect as well. Valuable insights and opportunities can arise when different strands of life come together in a new place. Because I'm far from home and have to make more of an effort to fit in, I've pursued activities here in Dublin that I might not have bothered with if I'd stayed around Boston. I help coach my son's youth baseball team (yes, that's right, a baseball team), and I've been lending a hand as he begins his Boy Scout career in a local group.

Through these endeavors, I've met people who have made me feel welcome and have eased my transformation from soft-spoken Yank to pseudo-Dub. Some are people with extensive ties to the area, others are more recent blow-ins like myself. Together, though, we're helping form a sense of community that benefits everyone, especially our kids.

But this is all an over-analytic adult speaking, who may at times wax too nostalgic. Indeed, life is made up of memories, but you have to live in the present moment to produce them.

Where my son is concerned, his memories around our Shankill home, in south county Dublin, are piling up fast and furious. Everywhere he looks, he sees the markers of an emerging life that will, in years to come, trigger a unique set of recollections, which he will then pass on to his kids, whether he stays in Ireland or ends up back in Boston.

Of course, sometime around Brian's 16th birthday, I reckon, we'll have reached a point of no return. By then, the facts will be pretty clear: this Medford guy has raised himself a Dub!

Euro-Weenie, I'm A Weenie

A SHORT TIME AGO, I was granted my first Irish passport. This came about because the often-mythical granny from Cork - sure, don't all Irish-Americans have at least one in their closet - was in my case a flesh-and-blood reality.

Back in 1992, thanks mainly to the efforts of my wife, Madge Reardon's birth and marriage certificates were traced to a small parish church in Minane Bridge, 15 miles south of Cork City. My grandmother sailed for Boston soon after her wedding day in 1929 and the church has suffered a major fire since, so finding these crucial documents was no sure thing. (Irish law allows foreign nationals to claim citizenship through a native-born grandparent, in case you're interested.)

In the end, we had to settle for facsimiles authorized by the local priest, and those papers formed the bureaucratic underpinning of my successful (if somewhat belated) application for an Irish passport in 2004.

As a result, I am now, by extension, a naturalized citizen of Europe, and I can travel with ease through the 27 countries of the European Union.

So how does it feel to be coming home, as it were, to the land of my forebears (Cork and Sicily, to be precise)? And, perhaps more to the point, is there a tug in my soul between my native country and my adopted land?

First of all, I should say that my voluntary decision to up sticks for Ireland - which is, after all, an English-speaking country (of sorts) with strong historical links to Boston - doesn't exactly rank with the life-wrenching choices other immigrants have *had to* make over the years, either out of economic necessity or to avoid persecution.

And to soften further any sense of culture shock I might feel, air travel from Dublin to Boston is now frequent and affordable, phone costs have come down significantly, and US imports - from TV shows to books to sporting influences - are thick on the ground here.

(In comparison, I have a good friend who left Boston for Texas 15 years ago and he still hasn't recovered from the shock.)

But this European dimension to my new identity has set me to thinking in a different direction altogether.

For starters, it just ain't hip to be a Euro-weenie these days. Effete government-dependent blowhards incapable of making a collective decision to save their lives – that's us. (Sorry, *them*.) Forget the preceding centuries of exemplary civilization Europe provided the world. When it comes to Europe these days (old Europe, anyway), you're talking about nothing but a bunch of opportunistic moaners and malcontents.

And those are some of the countries the US is still friendly with.

Getting away from any ideological antagonisms between Uncle Sam and his Old World counterparts, it's clear that Europe is going to need me – and countless other new recruits – in the coming years. Young, free-thinking native Europeans are so busy repositioning themselves at the center of the universe that they're forgetting to, well, reproduce themselves.

Birth rates in Germany, France, and Italy have fallen below self-sustaining levels. If a steady flow of immigrants doesn't pour in (and soon), those societies will find themselves in an unsupportable position: too few workers trying to fund too many retirees.

In the US, it's often said that our grandkids will end up paying for any fiscal imprudence we care to indulge in today. In Europe there won't be any grandkids to carry the can.

But such elementary assessments aren't very fashionable here. It's the big ideas that count, and the biggest of them all at the moment is that the US (or more precisely, George Bush's America) is bad news for Europe and the world at large.

For instance, a recent Transatlantic Trends survey, conducted in nine EU countries, showed that 72 percent of Europeans disapprove of the President's handling of international affairs, and 59 percent think US leadership is undesirable. (This news item appeared in the *Irish Times* under the headline "Europeans unmoved by Bush charm drive", which reveals an interesting bias in itself.)

So what's a boy with a foot on either side of the pond to do?

I'm a simpering socialist weenie if I see sense in the government models at work in France, Germany, and Scandinavia. And yet if I defend the US against long-distance clichéd criticism – as I have done by dashing off the occasional letter and op-ed piece to the *Irish Times* – I run the risk of portraying myself as a capitalist stooge warmonger.

For the moment, anyway, I'll blame my grandparents for my identity crisis. If they'd only stayed put, in Cork and Sicily, life would be a whole lot simpler.

Woolly Irish Ways
Proving A Gradual Fit

~~~~~~~~~~

THE UNTROUBLED AMBIGUITIES OF IRISH life used to really annoy me.

From the time I moved here in 1992 and had to rely on a careless Dublin shipping company to help track the transatlantic passage of my freight container from Cape Cod to Ireland, I've let fly against the laid-back Irish mentality.

The woolly ways of my new compatriots come in many forms, ranging from the trivial to the serious. The list includes non-existent or misleading road signs; a decided disinterest in certain areas of law enforcement (most notably where corporate corruption and traffic regulations are concerned); and fuzzy-headed notions about political neutrality (which have yet to win me over).

But with another St. Patrick's Day approaching fast, I've come to think that the best way to avoid lifelong irritability is simply to "go native".

For example, when I first arrived here, I was amazed by the extent of the litter problem. Both in cities and around the countryside, carelessly-disposed debris - candy wrappers, soda bottles and cans, newspapers, cigarette packets, plastic bags - blighted the landscape. And for variety's sake, there'd be the occasional burnt-out car, clapped-out washing machine, or sprung-out sofa thrown into the mix.

With the recent introduction of a waste disposal charge - which means that homeowners and businesses now pay a separate local fee determined by the amount of garbage they generate - the problem seems to have got worse. Illegal dumping of household trash as well as industrial rubbish is escalating.

The echoes of a successful elementary school anti-litter campaign still ring in my ears, so I'm committed to finding a proper outlet for my own candy bar wrappers and water bottles, not to mention whatever household trash I'm unable to recycle. But as for seeing someone else's rubbish nestled into tree branches or bobbing along in a stream, it doesn't faze me anymore. (Nor many other people, it would seem.) In my eyes, excessive litter is now part of the "natural" Irish landscape.

I've undergone a similar conversion where traffic laws are concerned.

Chronic double-parking? As I've come to observe, an Irishman in control of a motor vehicle is an obstruction waiting to happen. (And yes, that's me, on occasion.)

Unsecured loads on the backs of speeding trucks? The only solution here is to outmaneuver them, since the police don't seem to take notice.

And as for unthinking drivers who barrel down local streets at school time, with kids and parents alike crowding the sidewalks and sometimes slipping onto the road? Again my reaction is: it's all just part of the way things work here. Without a cop in sight, I'll try to keep my own child safe and hope other parents do the same.

On the lighter side, constant tardiness is regularly cited as a kind of genetic Irish flaw. Nothing starts on time in Ireland - according to the popular truism, anyway – and latecomers are allowed to charm their way out of any difficulty, or they might fall back on their reputation as an amusing eccentric.

I'm neither a charmer nor an eccentric, but like these self-styled "characters", I no longer get unduly worried if I'm going to arrive late for an occasion. I simply pull out my "Irish card" and remark jokingly to those I've left waiting: *Sure, I'm one of ye now!*

Of course, there's a fundamental reason for my going native, and it has to do with size. In a society as small and interwoven as Ireland's, every transaction eventually comes down to the personal level. Tip O'Neill had it right when he said that all politics are local. And none more so than the Irish variety.

It's no small coincidence that in years past, the city governments in Boston, Chicago, and New York have all been a little bit shady, and all a little bit Irish. By which I mean, deeply involved on the personal level, with favors exchanged for votes (and power) as a matter of course. Irish politicians - the successful ones, anyway - don't do the vision thing.

That's why a zero tolerance approach to law-enforcement (or indeed general tardiness) will never work here. Sooner or later, such an approach will affect you, someone in your family, or someone you work with. In other words, decent law-abiding citizens who deserve to be cut some slack.

To some, my live-and-let-live attitude might suggest a picture of near lawlessness. Superficially perhaps. Below the surface, Ireland enjoys a degree of social cohesion that other countries might learn from. But you have to live here and play by the rules - rather than just study how the nation's statute books are applied - to appreciate it.

Why Europe Doesn't Get Patriotism

~~~~~~~~~~~~~~~

As MY FIFTEENTH SUCCESSIVE FOURTH of July in Ireland approaches, I find myself asking: why doesn't Europe get patriotism? It's a simple enough question, but the answer is not so straightforward.

Europeans have no problem understanding nationalism. You can look at any period of European history - from medieval to modern - to see how nationalist movements have blighted the continent in the past.

What I'm referring to is the kind of plain, public-spirited pride that goes on display every year in the US on July 4th.

After a decade and a half away from my Boston home, it's my impression that America's Independence Day celebrations are indeed different. They lack the sense of insularity and exclusion that tinges similar festivities in Europe, whether it's Bastille Day in France or the commemoration of the 1916 Easter Rising here in Ireland.

Political figures from the extreme right in Europe are well able to spot this difference. And not just in the Balkans or the newly-liberated states of the old USSR, where poverty and economic crisis are often the norm.

In prosperous countries such as France, for example, Jean-Marie Le Pen still attracts a double-digit percentage of the vote in national elections, and far-right parties have been in government recently in Austria, Italy, Denmark, and the Netherlands.

Sinclair Lewis may have warned in his 1935 novel *It Can't Happen Here* that an even more dangerous swing to the far right could occur in the US, but I have my doubts.

Despite the Bush Administration's understandable obsession with national security, insularity, on the whole, is not the American way - even though US citizens are regularly accused of being out of touch with the rest of the world. Because of our history and our geography, Americans will always be looking out, to other shores and to other peoples.

Indeed, the majority of us are able to trace our origins to someplace else, and for many US citizens, reconnecting with our forebears - millions of whom fled an impoverished European homeland - can be a lifelong quest. (My own two sets of grandparents arrived in Boston around 1930 from Cork and Sicily.)

For this fundamental reason, Europeans just don't get US-style patriotism, which is based on an extraordinary set of foundation documents as well as a genuine national identity shared by all citizens, no matter where else they might call home.

Despite the European Union's clumsy efforts at producing its own defining *raison d'être* through a ponderous constitution and unwieldy institutions, Europe will never realize a similar ambition. Europeans will always consider themselves Italian, French, or indeed Irish, first and foremost, and any attempt to forge a more comprehensive identity extending beyond national borders will always falter as result.

This does not bode well for the future of Europe, according

to Professor John Gray from the London School of Economics. In his 2002 essay "The Dark Side of Modernity: Europe's New Far Right", Gray observes: "European institutions cannot replace national identities, but they are widely perceived as eroding them. Weakened national cultures do not cope well with the difficulties of assimilating newcomers; they are breeding grounds for a vicious populist politics that seeks to buttress identity through ethnic exclusion."

In the US, in contrast, the door to outsiders, slammed shut so forcefully in the aftermath of 9/11, is showing signs of opening once again, even though the Senate recently rejected a wide-ranging Immigration Reform Bill. Despite this setback, contenders for the presidency in 2008 will no doubt be asked to address this vital national issue in a meaningful way.

So despite the difficulty that has come of late with being an American in Europe, I'll celebrate with pride as the Fourth rolls around this year.

And even if our national day has its over-hyped and exploitative side, I'll remember the Declaration of Independence and the Constitution and the Founding Fathers. They have no equal here in Europe and might not for some time to come.

Sometimes, Eating Out
Is No Picnic

OVER THE LAST DECADE OR SO, Ireland has undergone a transformation unmatched among European nations - I'm speaking in economic terms here - and the ensuing prosperity has bestowed many blessings.

For instance, in the fifteen years I've lived here since moving from Boston, I've seen an unprecedented investment in infrastructure and social services, the return of past emigrants and an influx of new arrivals. Amid these undoubted benefits, however, there's at least one downside: the appearance of far too many trendy, overpriced restaurants.

That's my impression, anyway, and it was confirmed recently when I read a report in the *Irish Times* about the publication of the *2008 Bridgestone 100 Best Restaurants* guide, co-authored by culinary couple John and Sally McKenna. (I knew I was in trouble when I saw a particular establishment being complimented for capturing the *zeitgeist*.)

Time was when you couldn't pass through any village in Ireland - no matter how small or remote - without stumbling into a pub. Now you can't open a newspaper or magazine without tripping over a review of the latest restaurant sensation.

I try to read these articles, hoping to both educate and amuse myself, but unlike an actual meal, I can never quite finish them. The jargon of the professional diner and the arcane terminology given to simple meat and vegetable dishes, soon have me scratching my head in bewilderment.

For this reason - as well as my colossal ignorance where cooking is concerned - I seldom enjoy dining out these days. Even if the hostess is sufficiently impressed to allow me into her establishment, I often feel like a culinary illiterate once the menu arrives.

For instance, I've culled the following items from a recent restaurant review: arbequena shavings, marinated spatchcocked quail, and - the *piece de résistance* - gravadlax cured with salt and dill.

Now be honest. Without running to a dictionary of food terms, do you have any idea what these words describe?

There's also the question of service. Perhaps because of the country's colonial past, many Irish people have come to regard service economy jobs as an affront to their hard-won independence, and they can still put up a hardy resistance should they find themselves waiting tables, for instance.

(In fairness, this is partly down to the fact that Irish diners have yet to buy into the whole concept of tipping. Menu prices are so steep, they reckon, that good service is part of the deal - at no extra charge. As a result, gratuities, when offered, can be downright miserly, leaving wait staff with very little to play for.)

Another phenomenon hitting the Irish hospitality industry, noted by John McKenna at the launch of his guide, is that fewer native Irish people are entering the trade, at ground level anyway, so new vacancies are being filled by Eastern European and Chinese workers. In these cases rudeness isn't the issue, but rather the likelihood that you'll encounter interesting but decidedly non-Irish accents when it comes to transacting your culinary business at table level.

(This absence of the traditional "Irish welcome" in hotels and restaurants surprises many visiting traveler - Americans especially.)

As for the last item in my self-styled review of the Irish restaurant scene: there simply aren't enough reasonably-priced, middle-of-the-road eating establishments for unadventurous diners like myself who simply want to escape their own kitchens every now and again. We're not looking - in the words of John McKenna - for a "maverick" restaurateur who's willing to "do their own thing cooking with their own signature". Nor are we looking for "people who are defining the zeitgeist". Foodwise, anyway.

In contrast, when I return home, I really enjoy eating out in the small neighborhood breakfast joints around Cambridge and Somerville, where the menus are written in plain English and the waitresses are likely to address you as "hon" or "sweetheart". Without a hint of sarcasm, I might add. Also, the décor in these often family-run restaurants is homely, in the best sense of that word - unlike the minimalist approach favored by Dublin's more fashionable bistros.

As important, waiters and waitresses around Boston understand something that seems to have eluded their Irish counterparts. It's not a crime to have fun in your job, no matter how physically demanding it might be, and it pays to be courteous and efficient. Often in a big way.

Of course, just as any self-respecting writer might be expected to react negatively to criticism of his work, I'm sure that after reading this, many hard-working Irish restaurant employees wouldn't mind seeing me fall onto my steak knife. And then have a bottle of the house red poured over me.

Fair enough. But they'd be the ones staying on after their shift to clean up the mess.

My Sure-Bet Lottery System

LIKE MANY PEOPLE, I HAVE my own particular system for playing the lottery. The difference is that mine pays off every time.

What's my secret? Every Wednesday and Saturday, the two days on which numbers are drawn here in Ireland, I walk right past my local lottery outlet and pocket the nearly seven euros (now worth about $10) that it would take to play a basic combo ticket. In the past decade, I reckon I've "won" more than seven thousand euros as a result of my strategic penny-pinching. Not enough to retire on, mind you, but a heart-warming sum nonetheless.

I like to call my approach the "Anti-Lottery".

Here are the ground rules: if you play the lottery regularly each week, using a pre-determined set of numbers, those lines are no doubt etched in your mind. Your lucky numbers might signify important birth dates or anniversaries, and you're probably able to recite them without a moment's hesitation, like a child savant asked to unravel a difficult mathematical puzzle.

That was me, when I first moved to Ireland. Twice a week I played two lines of numbers that even now I can recite like my own name. These days I no longer play, but still - twice a week - I match those numbers against the winning lines generated by the National Lottery here. Then I breathe a massive sigh of relief when - invariably - my numbers don't come up.

The thrill is the same as if I'd actually played, but the odds are considerably greater in my favor.

If you think this system is ludicrous, consider the alternative. Lotteries everywhere play on the common fantasy of a single enormous payday that will ease all of life's problems. Here in Ireland, the allure of such a scheme is even more compelling. All lottery winnings are awarded in one tax-free, lump-sum payout. If you win the weekly minimum of 1.3 million euros, for instance, that's exactly what you get - no strings attached, no taxman knocking at your door for his cut of the action.

Of course, there are strings attached to every lottery win. And the strings get more intricate and more constricting in direct proportion to the size of your windfall.

Consider the case of Dolores McNamara, the Limerick woman who in the summer of 2005 scooped a Euromillions jackpot of 115 million euros, or roughly $170 million. The director of the Irish Lottery claimed it was the largest prize ever, anywhere in the world, since it was awarded in a single, tax-free payout.

Ms. McNamara comes from a modest enough background, judging from press reports, and her immediate response was to take herself and a planeload of her family and friends off to Spain for a holiday.

But after her Spanish getaway was over, she had to return to "normal" life. Just try to imagine the seismic effect that kind of instant, inconceivable wealth must have on a person's day-to-day routine. Ms. McNamara, to her credit, insisted on remaining in her working-class Limerick neighborhood. But to make that possible, a state-of-the-art security system had to be installed around her house. Also, one of her nephews had to flee the city because rumors spread that he might be kidnapped by local criminal gangs intent on securing a sizable ransom.

Now, having said all that, I wouldn't refuse a bit of good fortune should it come my way - a windfall of a few thousand euros would suit me just fine. In other words, a tidy enough sum so that I might get maybe a year ahead of myself, in financial terms, while remaining tethered to the mundane demands of ordinary life.

Still, for the moment, I'll continue with the system that has served me so reliably in recent times, slipping past my lottery dealer each week with the quiet assurance of a man who knows he's backing a winner.

What's The World Coming To
When Our Money Is Managing Us?

BACK IN MY YOUNGER DAYS, when I worked at Royal Books on Cape Cod and cut grass part-time, I had a pretty basic arrangement where money was concerned. Every week I'd earn a little bit of it and, just as regularly, through various transactions, it would end up in the hands of other people.

All very simple and straightforward.

There was no need for any smooth-talking advisors or helpful booklets or weekend seminars designed to show me how a property investment in some emerging backwater could be the key to my long-term financial security.

But then marriage and a child came along, and suddenly it was important that there was enough money tucked away for a rainy day and maybe even a week in the sun as well. Pension plans and retirement funds became hot topics, instead of being the conversational staple of windbags and old-timers.

And to top it all off? Thanks to the global economy, those of us within a slightly graying demographic now have international finance to worry about - which, as far as I understand it, involves prime lending rates, the price of various commodities, and the cost of a barrel of oil. Apparently, these all have the power to impact on my standard of living, which makes me think I should maybe take an interest.

But lately another thought has entered my head: you could spend a lifetime trying to make sure that your money is always putting in its best effort on your behalf.

These days, the guys in the know keep telling us that it's not enough to have a basic low-yield savings account. Given the vulnerability of even the strongest economies to inflation and recession, the truly wise and insightful among us are those investors, large and small, who know how to send their money out into the world. So that it might be fruitful and multiply. Via mutual funds and pension accounts and property deals. And then return home safely, for a while, before being sent out again on another lucrative mission.

In present-day Celtic Tiger Ireland - formerly branded as the Land of Saints and Scholars - there's a bit of a mania about the whole thing. It's difficult to express a thought, publicly or in private, in which money does not figure.

On television and radio, in pubs and on the street, the talk revolves around the price of property and the cost of living. This is because Ireland's financial gurus are advising us *ad nauseam* to change our phone service, switch banks, and juggle our stock portfolios. Frequently and without delay. All to save a few bucks. (Or in this case, a few euros.)

As well, the national dailies here regularly feature reports analyzing property developments in Spain, the US, Eastern Europe, and even China, which are now within reach of the average Irish investor. (Ironically, it is the average Irish investor who is seen as pricing the local folks in some countries out of their own housing markets.)

This new-found prosperity isn't a bad thing in itself. More than most other Western countries, Ireland needed an economic boost. But at what point, I find myself asking, does our money begin to manage us? At what point does the careful maintenance of our wealth become the principal concern in our lives?

I know what you're probably thinking: *Lighten up. We all have to make a buck and pay the bills.* This is true. Plus, on a personal level, I know I could conduct a comprehensive review of my own financial holdings over a breakfast meeting. And still have time to discuss the previous evening's ballgames at some length.

I get the feeling, though, listening to the radio and watching TV, that only a fool would choose to adopt an indifferent approach to his money these days, one that doesn't involve a careful consideration of the bottom line at every turn.

But let me be clear here. I'm not advocating a willy-nilly attitude to personal finance. This approach has millions of Americans - and a worrying number of Irish - up to their eyes in debt. What I'm proposing is that we simply forget about our wallets for a while, that for a short time anyway we don't put a price tag on everything in our lives.

Only then might we be able to appreciate the bigger picture in front of us each day.

Spreading The Gospel Of Baseball

AFTER FOURTEEN YEARS, I THOUGHT I had licked the problem of being a blow-in here, someone permanently stuck on the outside looking in. In many ways, as the saying goes, I'm now more Irish than the Irish themselves. For instance, I have very relaxed notions about arriving on time for social engagements, and any ideas I may have about social reform - say, a better health service or improved public transport - are now tempered with a native's sense of resignation.

Where sports are concerned, however, I'll always be a Yank, and a Bostonian first and foremost. Sure, I love soccer and follow the fortunes of England's Premier League teams. I'm also intrigued by hurling and Gaelic football and never miss the All-Ireland Finals each September. But at the end of the day it's my hometown teams that really matter.

This is especially true at this time of year, the beginning of the 2006 baseball season, with my hopes riding high for another (unlikely) Red Sox championship. But before you shed a tear for this thwarted fan, stranded thousands of miles from Fenway Park, wait a moment. Believe it or not, baseball is here, on the ground, in Ireland, having taken root among a dedicated core of players and coaches.

As this spring's inaugural World Baseball Classic demonstrated, America's national pastime has branched out over the past several decades, with enough talent now spread across the Caribbean and the Far East to put together a legitimate international tournament.

Perhaps some day Ireland will field a respectable national team and join the festivities. At the moment, though, even with a sprinkling of American ex-pats on the roster - there are roughly 16,000 of us resident here, some ex-college athletes with Irish roots - the team still struggles even against weak European competition. (There is hope, however, that the game will benefit from a PR windfall when *The Emerald Diamond*, New Yorker John Fitzgerald's documentary about baseball in Ireland, is screened in cinemas here.)

But that's pie-in-the-sky thinking where Irish baseball is concerned. For now the game is being nourished at a grass-roots level and is helping to reconnect many displaced Americans and their kids with an invaluable piece of our national culture. I confess I lost touch with the game myself after I moved from Boston to Dublin in 1992. Even though the 1990s proved relatively successful for the Red Sox, I wasn't that interested. I had no computer then to keep in touch via the Internet, and TV coverage in these parts was non-existent.

Then in late 1998 I got connected and soon began reading the occasional Red Sox game report on-line. But the real spur to my rebirth as a fan came in the autumn of 2003 when I pledged a monthly fee to my local cable TV company. In exchange, they granted me access to NASN, the North American Sports Network. I subscribed a few hours before Game 7 of the Red Sox-Yankees American League Championship Series. Despite the heartbreaking extra-innings loss, I was hooked.

A few months later, I began thinking about introducing my son Brian to the game. A friend in the States, who had lived in Ireland, pointed me in the direction of the Greystones Mariners baseball club in Wicklow, which caters for all comers, children to adults. My son had by then attended his first Red Sox game at Fenway Park, and his baseball knowledge seemed to be increasing exponentially. (For the record, Brian is sports-mad, independently of his dad, and is willing to try his hand - and feet - at anything.)

When we reported for the first "training session", I had trouble keeping to the sidelines. I introduced myself to the woman in charge - an energetic and outgoing Californian on temporary work reassignment in Ireland - and soon we were a management team.

Since then my son has moved up a level and I've followed him. Preaching the gospel of baseball to a group of seven- to nine-year-olds, most of whom are unfamiliar with the terminology and even the basic rules of the game, can be dispiriting at times. The kids have to rely on the basic equipment we provide - most don't own their own glove, which is like showing up for soccer training without your cleats or shinguards - and after they leave us each week, none of them will play the game among themselves. Plus, they have no favorite players to mimic on the field because they will rarely, if ever, see the game played, either in person or on TV, by capable adult practitioners.

And yet my personal connection to the game - as well as the enjoyment it can bring when played under a carefree summer sky - carries me back each Wednesday afternoon to the town park in Wicklow that we share with wandering dogs and lounging teenagers and strolling retirees. Among our group are Irish, Dutch, Spanish, and American kids - all united for two hours a week under the welcoming banner of baseball.

Dad's Dream Only A
Quick Pitch Away

LATELY, I'M BEGINNING TO IMAGINE how Earl Woods must have felt when he first recognized that his young son Tiger possessed an exceptional aptitude for golf. Mixed with the exhilarating possibility that you've sired a champion is the daunting responsibility that comes with then having to nurture a rare and luminous talent.

Now, before I get too far ahead of myself here, let me make one thing clear: my eight-year-old son will never be in the running for a major golf title. In fact, as regards the game, my sentiments are more in line with those of Mark Twain - who once remarked that golf is a good walk spoiled.

My own dreams of vicarious sporting glory center on a wholly different patch of green. If my son ever achieves athletic distinction, I'm convinced, it will be on the baseball diamond. Wearing the emerald cap of the Irish National Team.

As dreams go, then - I think you'll agree - it's a fairly modest one. But one well within reach. In fact, my Earl Woods moment occurred earlier this summer, in a public park in Dublin, where my son and I attended a modest four-team baseball tournament that served as a warm-up for the Irish National Team prior to their departure for Belgium and the European Championships.

(Yes, thanks to former Dodgers owner Peter O'Malley, who donated $140,000 toward the project, there is a serviceable diamond of major league proportions in Ireland, as well as enough skillful players around to adorn it.)

As my son and I sat in our collapsible canvas armchairs on a small rise along the first-base line, taking in the fine summer weather and the high-school caliber play, an interesting thought entered my mind. With a bit of encouragement and a good few hours of practice, my lad could represent his country on the baseball diamond.

This prospect became a good deal more appealing after we chatted with a young guy we know, Gareth Donnelly, who catches and plays third base for Ireland. Gareth was an impressionable 10-year-old living in Toronto when the Blue Jays won consecutive World Series titles in 1992 and '93. Hence his continued infatuation with the game after his family returned home to live in Ireland.

Unfortunately, though, there are few enough Irish players who have come up through the ranks like Gareth, learning the game as a youngster and then graduating to the national team. As a result, the immediate strategy for Irish baseball is to "grandfather" in a number of Irish-American players to help anchor the squad. This practice - which allows foreign-born players to claim Irish citizenship through a grandparent and thus become eligible for the national side - strengthened the Irish soccer team considerably in the late 80s and early 90s. Consequently, Ireland qualified for successive World Cups in 1990 and '94.

Anyway, according to Gareth, the Irish team was heading to Belgium fully intent on winning the Group B Championship and thus qualifying for Group A play. Hearing Irish baseball promoted in such a positive way, I allowed my imagination to roam a bit. As it happened, the two European participants in the inaugural 2006 World Baseball Classic - Holland and Italy - emerged from Group A, the elite unit that Ireland would like to join. And perhaps top someday.

Stretching my powers of deductive reasoning to the max, I saw myself trotting off to the 2018 World Baseball Classic as father and mentor to Ireland's ace pitcher (and slugger – what the heck), Brian "Slingshot" Coronella, so named for the outstanding velocity (and startling unpredictability) of his most famous pitch.

Of course, I mentioned this crazy scenario to no one. Least of all to my son. The last thing he needs right now is for me to hijack his enjoyment of a simple game of catch or Wiffle ball on the road outside our Dublin home. For the moment, I'll defer the dreams I have for him, and take pleasure in watching him run around and make friends as he learns the game I still enjoy playing so much myself.

Because as every parent knows, it's a fine line between encouraging your son or daughter in their athletic exploits and wanting to step back on to the field with them yourself.

If Facts Don't Fit, Irish Can Forget Their Past

~~~~~~~~

FOR A PEOPLE WHO ARE able to nurse a grudge for a century or longer (and make the dispute seem as fresh as the day it began), the Irish have an astonishingly brief memory where their economy is concerned.

As any recent visitor to Ireland will tell you, the country has been re-made over the past decade. Roads, buildings, even the natives themselves have undergone an extraordinary transformation.

But if you listen to the radio - as I regularly do, being at home most days - it soon becomes apparent that no one here, save a few antiquated begrudgers, cares to recall the dark days of the 1980s and even early 1990s. (Not to mention the forties and fifties, which weren't exactly Golden Eras either.)

I first visited Ireland in July 1980, with my mother and grandmother. At the risk of offending my Dublin neighbors and my Irish relations in Cork and Boston, the place seemed downright Victorian back then. It rained for three solid weeks, which meant that in most houses an open coal fire was burning, both to heat the premises and provide hot water via a back boiler behind the fireplace.

The effect, for me, was startling. No matter where I traveled - Cork, Dublin, or Galway - a gray sooty pall was the prevailing motif. Add to this a clear absence of any kind of civic or commercial vitality - outside of the pub, that is - and you get a pretty grim picture. (As I say, this isn't meant to offend anyone, but the fact that emigration was about to escalate sharply shows that even the Irish themselves didn't like what they were seeing.)

Listening to opposition politicians now, though, as well as to radio phone-in shows, you'd think that Ireland always possessed the vibrant economy it does today. This is especially apparent in the regular criticisms leveled at the health service.

Given that Ireland is indeed awash in public money, raised through corporate and individual taxation (but also through significant claw-back schemes targeting tax evaders over the past two decades), you'd be inclined to expect more from the public services here. And most people do – but are they being realistic?

For instance, tales of elderly patients waiting several hours - sometimes even days - on gurneys and armchairs in hospital emergency wards regularly feature in the papers and on the radio. The resulting outcry is clearly articulated and seemingly justified. People see the outward signs of a thriving, modern economy wherever they look, with apartments and office blocks springing up in every derelict lot, and they've come to expect a health service which is the equivalent of that in France or Canada.

But five decades (or more) of infrastructural neglect is not remedied overnight. And this is precisely where the Irish penchant for collective amnesia kicks in.

I like to cite a telling set of statistics that illustrates just how far Ireland has come in a very brief time. When I moved here in 1992, unemployment was running at 17 percent and mortgage rates were a crippling 14 percent. (Both are now under five percent.) In most countries, those figures would have been a recipe for revolution. But in Ireland, such numbers were the norm. (Even so, the World Bank was alarmed by Ireland's fiscal ineptitude in the mid-1980s and threatened to move in and run the place themselves.)

Perhaps the weirdest indicator of Ireland's warp-speed economic improvement, though, is the fact that quite a few people are now driving around in luxury cars that cost as much as a modest house did 10 years ago.

So, if a country is a basket case one decade and then finds itself producing economic figures that are the envy of Europe the next, is it reasonable to assume that its health and education systems, say, will experience a similar transformation in so short a time?

Well, not really. As I've mentioned, chronic under-investment over the years has had often irreparable effects. Almost all of Dublin's major hospitals, for instance, need to be leveled to the ground and rebuilt, rather than renovated - but where would the necessary back-up facilities come from in the interim?

And Ireland's overstretched health care infrastructure isn't the only problem making life difficult for the old and the infirm. Medical professionals - especially nurses - are now in short supply, and the Irish system is kept running increasingly by nurses and doctors from countries where they are also desperately needed, such as India and the Philippines.

I agree that the political establishment here has a lot to answer for. (Routine pettiness and indecision, most notably, as well as an aversion to new thinking.) But given my brief recitation of historical fact, I find it puzzling that the Irish people are expecting so much, so soon from their institutions and leaders.

Is Homespun Irish Welcome On The Wane?

IF YOU'RE CONSIDERING A VISIT to Ireland this summer, you've probably been tempted by the prospect of finding some legendary "Irish hospitality".

In your mind, you see yourself stepping off the plane at Shannon Airport, retrieving your luggage, picking up your rental car, and driving straight into the countryside. Before you collapse from jet lag, you chance upon a family-run B&B situated amidst rolling green hills and radiating a magical rural tranquility. The woman of the house appears to be expecting you. She welcomes you warmly at the door and asks in a genuine way about your visit. There is an aroma of fresh scones and tea from the kitchen.

Soon, you're on a first-name basis and it's almost as if the house is your own - you're given a key to the front door and told to come and go as you please.

It's an enticing scene, I know, but a vanishing one as well.

For starters, Ireland is becoming urbanized at an incredible pace, with all the leveling effects of such a process. Already, nearly one-third of the Republic's population of four million resides in the greater Dublin area, which, practically speaking, encompasses large parts of several adjoining counties. And a further half million are expected to swell this expanding commuter belt by 2020.

As a result, reaching some genuine Irish countryside in your rental car will take longer than you imagined. Or indeed, you may end up bypassing the rural experience altogether. Many of Ireland's smaller towns now have roads that run *around* them, so that you can zoom from, say, Galway to Cork, without having to slow down (and perhaps stop) in the less celebrated communities along the way.

But should you decide to follow your dream and find that enchanted countryside B&B, you'll find yourself in a select minority. According to figures published by the Central Statistics Office here, a vast majority of visitors from the US and Canada are spending their accommodation dollar on alternative digs. For instance, of the 8.7 million Irish "bed nights" registered by North American tourists in 2006, only 1.5 million (or 17 percent) were attributed to the B&B sector.

There are a few reasons for that scant percentage. First, B&Bs are not the inexpensive option they once were. (In my backpacking days I often secured a night's lodging, including breakfast and a friendly chat, for under $20. Today's budget traveler would be looking at $75, minimum, given the dollar's weak standing against the euro.)

Plus, independent B&Bs now face stiff competition from the many new three and four-star hotels that have sprung up around the country, owing to the generous tax breaks for such investment. These faceless franchise hotels feature pools, gyms, and saunas, as well as wireless Internet access, and regularly advertise cut-rate getaway deals.

But perhaps more seriously, from the perspective of a struggling B&B operator, the old-time Irish welcome is perceived to be on the wane - if one believes the anecdotal evidence presented on the radio phone-in shows here.

There has always been a certain craftiness behind the carefree Irish demeanor, but with Irish life becoming increasingly stressful, it appears that fewer people are interested in keeping up appearances - most notably in the B&B industry. Not when the paying overnight customer is now taking his business elsewhere. And not when the rewards for running a good B&B don't even come close to providing adequate recompense for the time and effort required.

So where does this leave your dream of an idyllic Irish vacation? Well, as I like to say, 20 years ago Ireland was a better place to visit; today it's a better place to live. In other words, if you come here for a visit, don't expect to find yourself transported to some mystical land of yore. Irish children aren't all red-haired and freckle-faced, no one lives in a thatched cottage anymore, and the pace of life, you'll discover, is remarkably similar to the one you left behind.

But if you get off the beaten track and explore some of the roads and byways that have yet to feel the hard brush of modernity, you'll be pleasantly surprised. And isn't that what travel is all about? Leaving your expectations at home and taking what the world has to offer.

Surely, that type of approach is deserving of a welcome anywhere.

Getting In Step
With Ancient Ireland

~~~~~~~

THIS YEAR MARKS MY SIXTEENTH consecutive St. Patrick's Day in Ireland. I'm sure a lot of Boston Irish could make a similar claim, but what sets me apart is that I've been resident here for that time. So you might think, reasonably enough, that I've developed a native's appreciation of Irish customs and practices.

Well, sort of.

As I've noted on numerous occasions to friends and family back in Boston, the institutions of a modern civic society don't always suit life in Ireland. In defiance of the countless European Union directives that come flying out of Brussels each week, the Irish people have remained resolutely tribal and stubbornly inward-looking in many ways. (And not just on the northern end of the island.)

It's been my experience that for better or for worse, anonymous social transactions are difficult to pull off here. Ireland is a pretty small country, after all. As a result, every transgression - and indeed every achievement - is magnified. And this produces a rich undercurrent of rumor and gossip in every town and village. (Indeed, even in cosmopolitan Dublin, pub chats and street corner exchanges can contain the most scandalous news.)

Sounds all very closeted and claustrophobic, which it can be at times. But perhaps a clannish mentality isn't always a bad thing.

These thoughts came to mind recently as I was preparing for another St. Patrick's Day by dipping into some early Irish history, specifically the dawn of the first millennium AD. This was when the Brehon Laws - so called because they were administered by the *brithemain*, or judges, who presided over individual clans - ruled the land.

In these so-called enlightened times, we tend to turn up our noses at outdated, often barbaric social systems from the distant past. One look at the basic precepts of Brehon Law, however, should make us think twice about rushing to such judgment.

For instance, one could argue that as a consequence of St. Patrick's introduction of Christianity into Ireland, communal liberties that existed under the Brehon Laws were eradicated. The position of women under the Laws, most notably, was comparable to that of men, particularly where marital break-up was concerned.

This led to an inevitable clash of values.

Owing to their remarkably modern divorce laws, which made formal provision for the divorced wife as well as the children of a second wife or those resulting from an extra-marital dalliance, the Irish kings and their legal system stood condemned abroad. Their principal accusers were members of the Catholic hierarchy on mainland Europe.

And the Brehon way was ahead of its time in another area of social justice. According to John O'Beirne Ranelagh, writing in *A Short History of Ireland*: "The Laws rarely resorted to capital punishment, preferring instead an elaborate compensation system, which also had the benefit of preventing long vendettas and establishing the law as the preferred arbitration procedure."

Only in cases where the offender defied all the injured party's petitions could the old rule of direct retaliation be used.

This system also seems to have fostered a form of protest common to this day in Ireland. Under the Brehon Laws, aggrieved parties could compel those of superior rank to deal with them by undertaking a hunger strike. "This procedure was held in some awe," John Ranelagh continues, "and it is clear that great dishonour fell upon a defendant who refused to submit to it."

Of course, no set of laws is perfect, and the Brehon system had its flaws. For example, the family was the recognized legal unit in ancient Irish society, and this determined forever one's standing in life. Social mobility was non-existent, and any mention of individual freedoms or rights was still centuries away.

Also, as Sean Duffy points out in his informative study, *Ireland in the Middle Ages*: "Our mental picture of Ireland in the seventh and early eighth centuries is clearer and far more detailed than that available for almost any country in Europe." Where the Brehon Laws are concerned, this leads him to observe: "As in today's world, the theory of the law is often contradicted by the reality of practice."

So do we have anything to learn from the old Irish law texts set down over a thousand years ago and which survive to this day? Well, maybe that's what St. Patrick's Day festivities can be about in future. We can sideline the shamrocks and the Guinness and instead get in step with the sense of justice and fair play embodied in the Brehon Laws.

The Summer Of My Irish Commune

~~~~~~~~~~

A COUPLE OF MONTHS BACK, I posted off the deposit for a week's rental on Cape Cod in August. As I see it, handing over money in this fashion is a sure sign that summer is just over the hill and around the next bend.

But the transaction also recalled a previous, supposedly short-term Cape sabbatical, kicked off in June of 1986, which only came to a close when I moved to Ireland six years later.

Here's how events unfolded. The day after Christmas in 1985, three friends and I hopped on a plane and paid a much-anticipated visit to the Old Sod. (As it turned out, getting to Ireland was almost as much fun as being there, involving as it did an early morning train ride from Boston to New York, a subway trip out to Terminal Five at JFK, and our eventual disembarking at Shannon Airport outside Limerick.)

After we recovered from our jet lag - not to mention our introductory breakfast, which included several lashings of some vintage Bushmill's whiskey - we jumped in our rental car and made our way along many a dark and wet winter's road from Cork to Dublin, back to Cork, and over to Kerry. (If you check out a map of the 26 counties, you'll see that the distances involved are short enough. But in mid-1980s Ireland, in the belly of a Hibernian winter, these were challenging drives, requiring frequent stops to test the quality of the local Guinness.)

I remember that we celebrated New Year's Eve at the holiday home of a friend in Glenbeigh, on the Ring of Kerry. I also recall that a bit more drink may have featured once we reached our destination. This would explain why I wandered outside, at some point in the evening, to take some air and gawk at the star-packed night sky. After a few moments looking upward, I decided to go for a quick lie-down on the back seat of our rented Toyota Carina. I woke up sometime later and heard a general commotion. It seemed a search was on - for me. Unfortunately, the Toyota came equipped with a rear door child-lock mechanism, which, in my diminished state, I was unable to crack. Finally, after about half an hour, I was found peering out from behind a seriously steamed-up car window.

(Note to any of you young adults out there: find a nice fluffy bed to lie down on instead. And remember that your body is a delicate vessel, not an industrial-strength, brewery-standard holding vat.)

Anyway, our Yuletide excursion occurred during a time of profound economic uncertainty in Ireland, when a J-1 working visa was more sought after by Irish students than an honors degree in college. To take up the visa, however, US authorities required that Irish students submit a letter of sponsorship from an American citizen. This served to guarantee any applicant's well-being and upkeep in the event he or she was delayed in finding work.

Given these hard realities, our high-spirited holiday soon took a different turn. Dan, Joe, Jimmy, and myself became guarantors to about half a dozen Irish students who were interested in working on the Cape the following summer. And as Dan was already living in West Yarmouth, he promised to initiate a search for digs as soon as he returned home in

February - a move we all heartily endorsed, considering the outstanding welcome we'd received.

As it turned out, we were perhaps a bit hasty in trying to match our various hosts' hospitality by promising to set them up stateside come summer. I didn't return from my travels till May, having journeyed on to England and Italy, and I never saw myself joining the Cape commune anyway. Also, Dan's life had taken its customary twists and turns, so that as the mid-June deadline approached, he found himself scrambling around looking at potential rental houses.

In the end, Dan found a place that couldn't have been more suitable. It was centrally located, off Route 28 in South Yarmouth. Plus, it had an outdoor shower and a converted attic, not to mention a large living room with loads of floor space to accommodate some makeshift bedding. This would prove essential because the word from Ireland was that the number of interested parties was growing. I'd been persuaded to spend the summer on the Cape as well.

By the time the first recruits arrived at Logan Airport, we were well prepared for them - meaning we'd moved into the house and a handful of jobs had been secured. What followed over the coming weeks was a daily succession of minor whirlwinds, as about ten of us (on average) got up, showered, dressed, ate, and made our way to work on one of the several bikes parked outside the back door. In the evenings, the process was reversed.

The house also served as a kind of way station for Irish students - sisters, cousins, friends of friends, etc., - who needed temporary lodgings until they found a place of their own. We made a tally at the end of the summer and came up with the names of 40 wayfarers who had spent at least one night under our roof. In some cases, that was one night too many. And through it all, remarkably, the house itself bent but never broke.

We were, in fact, very good tenants.

I hope to have a more relaxed time on the Cape with my family in August. There'll be far fewer of us, for starters, and everyone is guaranteed a proper bed.

Still, when I signed the lease to secure our holiday house, I couldn't help smiling as I recalled "The Summer of My Irish Commune" on Cape Cod.

My Hometown Now Rivals
Any Vacation Spot

I HAVE A SIMPLE QUESTION for anyone now living out-of-state or in another country, hundreds of miles or even an ocean apart from the place they grew up in. What I'd like to ask is this: how long do you have to be living elsewhere before your hometown becomes as interesting and attractive as any of the world's more distant destinations?

The answer, in my case, is 16 years. That's how long I've been living in Dublin, Ireland, a voluntary exile from the humble surroundings of Medford, Massachusetts.

My new outlook materialized this past summer, during my family's annual stateside vacation, when I suddenly found that my hometown had shaken off the unflattering image I'd often had of the place: hard-edged, suspicious of change, sometimes dangerous.

Indeed, when presenting itself to the outside world, Medford has regularly been its own worst enemy. I can recall that when I was in high school, for instance, you'd admit to being from Medford as a prelude to a brawl, or as an excuse for a perceived lack of social graces. There's also the little matter of the FBI's only successful wiretap of a Mafia initiation ceremony - which took place years before *The Sopranos* in a house on the north side of the city - not to mention the notorious $25 million bank heist recounted so vividly in the 1987 book, *The Cops Are Robbers*.

And to top it off, our most celebrated literary son, Paul Theroux, writing about his Medford upbringing in a 1979 essay called "Traveling Home: High School Reunion", says: "I had good friends, but I was nagged by one thought: the world was elsewhere. I left Medford the first chance I had, and Medford became part of the dark beyond, as I converted my memories into fiction."

These days, though, according to freelance journalist Ed Siegel, who resides in Medford, the place is known as "Funky Town", owing to its diverse and emerging cultural and culinary attractions.

The city has certainly changed in recent years. Medford now seems to be attracting another generation of immigrants - Asian, Caribbean, Hispanic - as once it lured the sons and daughters of Irish and Italian immigrants who'd grown up, like my own parents, in North Cambridge or Boston's West End neighborhood.

As well, Medford has become a desirable spot for many young professionals, who see its relatively quiet, settled streets as a good place to bring up their kids, a pleasant blend of urban and suburban, with house prices just about affordable and an easy access via bus and subway to downtown Boston. There's also the feeling of satisfaction that comes with living in a college town. (Tufts University is located on a hill overlooking the city.)

The curious part for me, though, is where I now fit in this picture. I'm no longer an insider, nor am I an innocent blow-in. Luckily, my present status, uncertain and ill-defined, has helped me to see Medford from a fresh perspective. This became apparent during a leisurely outing back in August on the Mystic

River, which I found still courses rather sluggishly through my hometown. (Some things never change.)

My brother-in-law Mark is a professional mechanic and keen boating enthusiast, and it was thanks to him that my young son and I enjoyed a delightful jaunt aboard his 18-foot outboard. The compactness of the craft, as we headed out on the river, under a succession of bridges, toward Somerville, Everett, Chelsea, then the sea, made the journey all the more exciting. I couldn't help feeling as well that I'd become something of a tourist in my own backyard.

From the middle of the river, it was easy to imagine Medford's illustrious 19th-century maritime history, a time when Clipper Ships built in local yards sailed the world carrying another famous Medford product: rum. As Mark steered us past the many boats still moored on the Mystic ("No Wake When Passing" warned sign after sign), I made a mental note to find out more.

But it wasn't just the distant past that piqued my interest.

After motoring along for a bit (and briefly enduring the rattle and hum of Interstate 93 as we passed beneath it), we slowed for a closer look at the recently-built elementary and middle schools located in an unlikely spot near Hormel Stadium, headquarters of the Medford Mustangs high school football team.

I recalled from past visits that the construction of these large ultra-modern facilities was a matter of some controversy, resulting ultimately in the closure of several older neighborhood schools that were in need of expensive repairs.

From the river, the schools looked up-to-date all right, and very big, which made me think - as the critics have suggested - that it might all seem a bit daunting to a five or six-year-old just starting out.

Farther along, we passed under the distinctive green lattice-work of the Mystic Tobin Bridge on our way out to Boston Harbor. Traversing this busy channel, we bobbed in the wake of pleasure craft more powerful than our own, as well as larger cruise vessels catering to tourists. We even ventured out to the mouth of the harbor, where it feeds into more serious waters. Here we paused to gawk at one or two planes, just barely above us, landing noisily at Logan Airport.

By the time Mark piloted us back to dockside in Medford, we'd been on the water for almost two hours. And though I didn't realize it at the time, it is only now - after 16 years of happy exile - that I am beginning to appreciate the town I left behind.

What If Ireland Really Was The 51st State?

~~~~~~~~

FOR A MISPLACED AMERICAN SUCH as myself, living in Ireland during a US presidential election can be an enlightening experience.

Ever since the Democrats and Republicans endorsed their respective candidates a few weeks back, Irish commentators have gone to town in the analysis department. Whether the forum is the op-ed page of the major dailies or the sound-proofed confines of a broadcast studio, they've been pontificating long and hard on what a McCain or Obama Administration will mean for America and the rest of the world. (Answer: either more of the same or something hopefully different.)

The tone of these discussions can vary, from smug and dismissive to affable and insightful. But beneath all the speculation and scrutiny surrounding our imminent presidential showdown, there's an interesting subtext.

It's a given here that Ireland and her people enjoy a special status within the US political establishment. Indeed, most congressional leaders and presidential hopefuls - if they're on their game - will confess to having Irish roots. And not just on St. Patrick's Day.

But one also gets the impression, listening to Irish observers, that the Republic would compare favorably, as the 51st member of the Union, with the more progressive US states, those beacons of reasonably enlightened governance such as Minnesota, Washington, or Oregon.

Sorry, but I'm not even sure Ireland would find a home among the six New England states, which include countless towns and cities colonized by Irish immigrants over the years.

In fact, the evidence suggests that Ireland would be located more comfortably in the conservative Midwestern heartland, and might even spill over a bit into the Bible Belt. If you think I'm just a cranky ex-pat letting off steam after eight years of an impossibly frustrating government back home, I'd ask you to consider the following:

☐ State-supported church schools are something US Republicans would die for. Well, in Ireland, 99% of primary schools remain under the management of either the Catholic or Protestant Churches. If you're a social democrat, which is a label the majority of Irish people would gladly wear, this has many obvious and unsettling implications. Maybe calling oneself Catholic or Protestant has become a simple badge of convenience in modern Ireland, but the fact remains that the administration of nearly all Irish elementary schools rests in the hands of a self-selecting few. This would not be a vote-getter in those US states most Irish commentators see as their spiritual home.

☐ Abortion and same sex marriage are prohibited in Ireland. Whatever one's personal position on these matters, the fact that the Irish state outlaws them places the Republic squarely in the McCain/Palin camp. And dare I mention that homosexuality was *decriminalized* in Ireland only about a decade ago?

☐ Ireland's centralized government bureaucracy - from education to health to justice - would do any Eastern bloc regime proud. When it comes to problem-solving, the Irish Civil Service can see no difference between a struggling rural township in County Donegal and a distressed inner city neighborhood in Cork or Dublin. There is no room - on a practical or imaginative level - for addressing the unique needs of each community. And with very little of their own revenue to work with, local County Councils are just as constrained. This is a feature of Irish life that US citizens from both blue and red states - who are used to electing city councils and school committees with their own budgets - would find problematic.

☐ Despite vigorous objections from other European Union states, Ireland is still able to entice foreign investment with an exceptionally attractive 12 percent corporation tax that even the most ardent US capitalist would regard with disbelief. (Before deciding to set up shop here, as many have.) John McCain has repeatedly promised that if elected, he'll lower corporation tax in the US to just over *30 percent*.

☐ And finally, the same political party, with the odd junior coalition partner, has been in power in Ireland for the past 11 years - and 19 out of the last 21 years. Though most Irish people would undoubtedly vote Democrat if given the chance, their domestic voting patterns hardly indicate an Obama-esque appetite for change.

Of course, if McCain & Company retain the White House in November, who am I to talk about turning over a new leaf?

Then And Now

Back When The Bruins Owned Boston

DESPITE THE RECENT SUPER BOWL blip in Arizona, these are great days to be a Boston sports fan. Last October the Red Sox won the World Series for the second time in four years, the Patriots had another great season - even if it wasn't perfect - and the Celtics are back to their winning ways at the Garden.

But the team I remember most vividly from my early days as a sports fan in the Hub - even though our relationship has faltered in recent years - is the Boston Bruins. It's hard to believe, I know, but in living memory the Bruins owned Boston. For a glorious half-decade or so beginning in the early 1970s - during my days as an elementary school student in Medford, if you're looking for a personal marker here - Boston belonged to Bobby Orr and his assorted cohorts. Along with the Boy Wonder from Parry Sound, there was Espo, Cheesie, Pie, and the Chief. Together, they brought a swashbuckling spirit to the local sports scene.

(Not to mention two Stanley Cups in 1970 and '72, the first of which produced perhaps the most memorable image in Boston sports history: Bobby Orr flying through the air in front of Glenn Hall's goal after scoring in overtime to complete a four-game sweep of the St. Louis Blues.)

As kids, we stayed up late to catch the Bruins' West Coast games on Channel 38, and then we'd watch them again on WSBK-TV's twice-weekly Bruins highlights show. But there was an even bigger spin-off from all this interest: we became avid street hockey players, like all the kids around Boston. (Playing on ice, in full equipment, was for serious enthusiasts.) Most of the time we played on hardtop streets, body-checking each other into people's front-yard bushes and using the curbs as our boards to jazz up our passing.

During the winter, though, we'd get lucky on occasion. After a storm, we'd let the snowplows do their work, then we'd pray that a hard-packed layer of snow and ice remained to allow for a fast-moving game. (Of course, we'd pray for a cold spell as well. Any bit of sun or even the slightest rise in temperature above 32 degrees, and we'd find ourselves slogging through a soupy mix of slush and sand.)

Back in those heady days, the kids I hung out with owned all the required street hockey gear, more than likely bought at Tony Lucci's in Medford Square - gloves, pads, folding metal nets, and any number of disposable Superblades (including the latest version for those who liked to tend goal, like myself).

Sure, there were arguments and flare-ups and disputed goals. But we settled it all ourselves: there wasn't an adult in sight.

And no one owned a second car back then, so the streets were clear all day. When the neighborhood dads came home from work in the early evening, they'd pull into the driveway, and we were able to keep playing - so long as the streetlights were strong enough and our patience with one another hadn't run out.

As I'm discovering when I sit down to watch the modern game, hockey has changed over the years. On the Barry Park basketball courts in Medford, for instance, I've seen kids charging "up-ice" on roller blades. As for the pros, they're faster and more skillful, and a good many of them now come from Russia, the Nordic countries, and Eastern Europe.

But no matter how much the sport may change, my hockey heroes will always be the motley crew of big names and journeymen chronicled in a 1969 book by Stan Fischler (which was on my Christmas list that year).

For me, hockey will always be the story of *Bobby Orr and the Big, Bad Bruins*.

Playing Nixon In School Debate Ensured I'd Never Run Again

EVERY TIME I HEAR BARACK Obama or John McCain answer a dumb question with an equally dim-witted response, I feel their pain. That's because I, too, have campaigned for the presidency of the United States and said some absolutely ridiculous things.

The year was 1972, and I was an awkward 13-year-old playing the part of Richard Nixon - against a female classmate's George McGovern - in a mock debate organized by our eighth-grade geography teacher at Lincoln Junior High School in Medford, Massachusetts.

To echo the tag line of the man I was chosen to represent, let me make one thing perfectly clear: I was a reluctant candidate for the nation's top job back in '72. The country was at war, an energy crisis loomed, and political campaigns were fast becoming an even dirtier and more dishonorable business. (Hmmm, sounds familiar.)

Plus, I was having some serious hair issues that would linger for another decade, and my public-speaking skills at the time would have made a cloistered monk seem chatty in comparison.

Given my obvious unsuitability for public office, how did I find myself pushing the Republican Party platform surrounded by a classroom full of Democrats-in-waiting? Well, in the tradition of politicians everywhere, I'd like to put the blame for my unfortunate circumstances on someone else. Specifically, a boyhood friend by the name of Mark Storella.

Mark and I had met in elementary school, and our friendship continued as we made the unsettling transition to seventh grade. After one year in the rough-and-tumble of junior high, however, Mark departed for a well-regarded private school. We remained in touch, though over time saw less and less of each other.

But when opportunity came knocking in the run-up to the Nixon-McGovern election, Mark - along with his Republican sensibilities - was there for me, urging me to take part in the democratic process. Junior high style, anyway. (It's worth noting that the primary system in 1972 was much more straightforward than it is today. Back then, it consisted simply of Mrs. Oosta, our eighth-grade social studies teacher, pointing in my direction and saying, "I think you should be our Nixon.")

To help me look the part, Mark was able to locate a sizable quantity of Nixon bumper stickers, campaign buttons, and policy pamphlets, which I still have. (I never asked Mark who his source was, but if you'll recall, the Nixon campaign team labored under the unfortunate acronym of CREEP, the Committee to Re-Elect the President. Not a good omen, as it turned out, for our 37th Chief Executive.)

All the Nixon literature was clearly written and very professional looking, and bespoke a candidate on the top of his game. I wish I could say the same for his frizzy-haired eighth-grade stand-in, whose dress sense, by the way, was more ragtag than Republican. I did experience a brief flush of confidence after studying the Nixon policy positions, thinking that if

I could master these, the debate would inevitably tilt in my favor.

I was wrong. On the morning of the debate, the butterflies started fluttering. In droves. And later in the day when I took my seat at the front of the class as Richard Milhous Nixon, my mouth dried up and my brain went into lockdown.

Also, the "George McGovern" I was facing had the advantage of being blonder and better-looking than me. She may have been wearing a miniskirt as well. And with the help of four or five other kids in the class who served as the impartial press corps assigned to grill us on the issues, she hammered me on a subject I couldn't shake: the Vietnam War.

In response to the panel's repeated questions about whether I, as Nixon, would send my own son to Vietnam, I could only splutter a red-faced rebuttal. Something along the lines of "War may not be nice, but someone's got to do it."

I have a vague recollection that there was a class vote taken at the end of our debate and that I lost by a landslide. (Which was an accurate reflection of the way Massachusetts voted generally in 1972. We were the one state, you'll recall, that McGovern carried, resulting in the classic bumper sticker: *Don't blame me - I'm from Massachusetts!*)

I've yet to seek counseling on the matter, but I sometimes think that my teenage impersonation of Richard Nixon is the reason why I haven't run for public office since. And why I never discuss presidential politics with women in miniskirts.

My Textbook *Non Sequitur*

~~~~~~~~~~~

IT'S FUNNY HOW THINGS WORK sometimes.

For instance, if Bobby Fischer hadn't traveled to Reykjavik, Iceland to take on Boris Spassky in the world's most celebrated chess match in the summer of 1972, I never would have got the chance to learn Latin at my junior high school in Medford, Massachusetts.

Sounds like a real *non sequitur*, I know, but hear me out.

For starters, you don't have to be a chess geek to remember the American grandmaster Bobby Fischer. In his time he elevated the game to unprecedented levels of popularity, thanks to his spectacularly bold play and dazzlingly eccentric behavior. (He died in 2007, aged 64, back in Iceland, a broken and embittered man.)

Anyway, after a lot of pre-match wrangling, mainly over prize money, Fischer agreed to meet Spassky for the World Chess Championship in the remote venue of Reykjavik. The first game took place on July 11, 1972.

I'm not exactly sure what my summer vacation routine consisted of back then, but it's a good bet that it included large amounts of what today would be called "unscheduled time".

As a result, I spent countless hours watching "World Chess Championship" on Boston's PBS affiliate, Channel 2.

Incredibly, the show - which featured grandmaster Shelby Lyman analyzing each game (and indeed each move) of the Fischer-Spassky contest - was at the time the highest-rated PBS program ever and yet had an endearing slapdash feel to it. The studio contained little more than a giant wall-mounted chess board, re-configured by Lyman after each new move would arrive via teletext, as well as a few seated chess pundits enlisted for their own powers of analysis.

Despite the cheesy production values, the show was an inspiration, and in September of '72 I entered the eighth-grade at Lincoln Junior High School convinced that I possessed the mental muscle to become the next great American chess champion. To condition myself, I stayed after school a couple of days each week to engage my English teacher, Mr. Kelly, in a series of friendly matches.

Mr. Kelly, I recall, had a similar enthusiasm for the game but unfortunately didn't appear to have benefited from the helpful advice offered by Shelby Lyman and company on PBS. He took forever to make a move, and when he finally did commit one of his pieces, it pushed him invariably closer to checkmate.

Between moves, I often got up and wandered around Mr. Kelly's classroom. One afternoon, I found myself examining the contents of the glass-paned inset bookcase at the rear of the room. An old Latin textbook caught my eye. I took out the dusty tome, which probably hadn't been handled for decades, read a few simple phrases, and committed them to memory.

The next time I met Mr. Antico, one of two guidance counselors at Lincoln and a notorious lover of languages, I blurted out those bits I could recall: *Britannia insula est.* (Or thereabouts. An *agricola* of unknown origin might have figured in there somewhere as well.)

It was an utterance that would change my life.

Mr. Antico was a big man and, perhaps indicative of his

Italian background, wasn't afraid of showing his emotions - especially when someone demonstrated even a rudimentary grasp of a language he adored.

He threw his right arm over my shoulders and pulled me toward him. "Ah, well done, *Stefanos rex!*" he said.

I should have known better.

For the next nine months at Lincoln, that was to be my calling card as Mr. Antico took me under his wing and tutored me in the quirky details of Latin grammar. At roughly 12:30 each afternoon, as the rest of my homeroom was settling into some free time, Mr. Antico summoned me over the class intercom. First came the unmistakable crackle of the mike being switched on in the school's main office. Then, "*Stefanos rex* to my office, immediately!"

Mr. Antico wasn't shy about issuing the odd proclamation either.

After a moment's hesitation, I'd look in the direction of our homeroom teacher, get her tacit approval to leave, and rise from my desk at the front of the room. Then I'd walk the longest walk of my life, past the smirks and giggles of my contemporaries - many of whom, I now suspect, were mystified by my privileged status.

With Mr. Antico as my guide, I spent many homeroom periods declining nouns and conjugating verbs of the Latinate variety, and without doubt my command of English improved as a result.

Later that year I gave up my dreams of chess dominance, but the Latin remained with me. Indeed, I took three years of it in high school and to this day the connection between the two is undeniable.

You could call it a classic case of *quid pro quo.*

Clutter Me Wonderful!
In Praise Of Souvenirs

NOTHING SIGNIFIES A WELL-SPENT holiday more than a suitcase full of souvenirs. Whether they're bought in Cairo or on Cape Cod, in New Delhi or Dingle, nothing says "I've been away!" more than those varied keepsakes - large and small, tacky or tasteful - that you simply must have to round off your annual getaway and which then proceed to take up space in a forgotten corner of your home once your traveling is done.

How do I know this? Because I've been there and bought the T-shirt - as well as a good few other trinkets along the way. I've surrendered to those same impulses, only to wonder months (or even years) later what I ever saw in that diminutive statue of a gondolier I picked up in Venice back in 1982.

During a second Italian trip, a few years later, I found myself in Rome, on my way to visit my father's family in Sicily. As one does when in the Holy City, I wandered over to St. Peter's Square, hoping to boost my spiritual stock, only to discover that the place was ringed with souvenir stands selling everything from papal dish towels to Vatican ashtrays. On this particular occasion, I showed commendable restraint, restricting myself to some celestial stationery, namely, a pen and note pad embossed with the beaming visage of a resplendent John Paul II.

Yes, I'm a sucker for souvenirs. After all, distinctive mementos like Guinness key chains and thatched cottage fridge magnets will never go out of style - since they were never fashionable in the first place.

Anyway, my reputation as a shameless hoarder of unmarketable collectibles was confirmed recently when I came across several boxes of knick-knacks and keepsakes from my modest travels in decades past. The treasure in question was unearthed during a spell of merciless closet de-cluttering.

The first item up for appraisal was a paper placemat from a Burger King in Madrid advertising the magnificent El Whopper. Apparently, I was so impressed by the linguistic versatility of the fast food industry that I also took away a placemat from a McDonald's in Geneva. Mind you, I never realized how cutting-edge these collectibles would become. Only a decade later, Quentin Tarantino would feed John Travolta his classic *Pulp Fiction* lines which, coincidentally, reveal an intimate understanding of French fast-food menus.

Of course, I didn't just eat my way - rather poorly - across Europe in those days. There was also culture, if the various theatre programs I accumulated are to be believed. According to the documentary evidence still on file in my closet, I saw a group called Harvey and The Wallbangers perform a musical revue called "Park The Tiger". This was in 1986, in the Belfast Opera House - I think. The program is unclear about the venue, which isn't surprising given the volatile political climate in Northern Ireland at the time.

I also saw some Beckett and Behan in Dublin, as well as a performance of *Glengarry Glen Ross* in the Mermaid Theatre in London. To offset the intensity of the David Mamet play, I then took in some lighter fare entitled *Lend Me A Tenor* at the Globe.

It might sound as though I'm flaunting my cultural

credentials here, but back then that was the farthest thing from my mind. Going to see a play or hear some live music was as much about killing time before I set off for the next city on my whistle-stop European backpacking tour.

What else could explain the fact that in an Avignon movie house, in southern France, I sat through a late showing of *Les Aventeurs de L'Ark Perdue* (*Raiders of the Lost Ark*) while waiting for a 2 am train to Italy. Or that, in similar circumstances, I slipped into a cinema in Rome to see *Rocky IV*. (Given the lack of sub-titles, the only line I was able to make out was "Bonna fortuna, Rocky".)

Without doubt, though, I picked up my two most meaningful keepsakes in a small town called Augusta on the east coast of Sicily. This is where my paternal grandparents were born. From my father's uncle Francesco I received a meticulous hand-drawn copy of our family tree (the Italian side, that is), which he entrusted to me with genuine care. And then, later in my visit, I found an oversize black-and-white postcard of the local church where my grandparents were married before they sailed for Boston. When I got home a couple of months later, I had the postcard mounted and framed, as a gift to my father.

As you can see, then, I'm the last person to utter an unkind word about souvenirs. Even the smallest keepsakes can evoke cherished memories from travels past.

But you have to be selective. Even I can't justify the 4-foot-high inflatable leprechaun I saw in a Dublin shop window the other day.

This Fashion Plate
Ready To Crack

~~~~~~~~~~

WHERE MY GENERAL APPEARANCE IS concerned, my wife insists that I remain "in style". To be fair, she isn't exercising her authority without good reason here.

Left to my own interpretation of current fashion and grooming trends, I'd soon turn into a walking, talking endorsement of the 1970s. Before you could say "Who's the geek so out of step with the times?", I'd be wearing checked flannel shirts and department store sneakers again and letting my hair adopt whatever style it damn well pleased. (Which, in my pubescent prime round about the Disco Era, was usually out to the sides in heavy layers, like a certain cynical clown out of *The Simpsons*, rather than flowing down to the shoulders, in a manner that today's young people seem to be favoring once more.)

So you can see why I tend to listen to fashion advice, from whatever quarter.

But that doesn't make it right.

For instance, I'll never understand how certain "styles"

evolve, and why some people dress and decorate themselves as elaborately as any native chieftain preparing for battle.

This fashion deficiency can't be accounted for solely by my gender - though men are more likely to emerge from the house in a crumpled or ill-matched ensemble. On the other hand, it is men, by and large, who are the fashion czars, dictating to the rest of us what constitutes hipness and what epitomizes unspeakably poor taste.

Of course, sometimes the two overlap, and for those with a sense of humor, the fashion catwalks can be a source of profound hilarity. The solemn demeanor of underfed and overindulged models parading about in wisps of silk and flourishes of cashmere - well, it's beyond parody, despite Ben Stiller's best efforts to lampoon the fashion scene in *Zoolander*.

And yet in Ireland, as in many otherwise sane jurisdictions, current clothing trends are given serious, even reverential treatment. For instance, during the annual celebration of Dublin Fashion Week, the newspaper of record here, the *Irish Times*, often devotes a sizable portion of its inner pages to the latest outbreak of "style" in the world of *haute couture*. This same slavishness to fashion extends to Irish TV as well, where the flagship weekly variety program, *The Late, Late Show* (which airs at 9:30 pm, by the way, hardly middle-of-the-night stuff), has got in on the act with their tedious Emerging Designer Competition.

And this is on top of the peculiar Irish custom of drafting in indigenous fashion models to publicize charitable causes or launch equally laudable fund drives. (It's surprising, actually, that a country as small as Ireland can maintain a ready supply of models for these frequent page-one photo ops.)

Getting back to my own sense of style - which, to be honest, exists solely on the microscopic level - it's apparent to me that men and women have very different ideas about fashion. For instance, men feel a sense of accomplishment if they're able to wear the same shirt for a week without creating a bio-hazard.

Women, on the other hand, insist on laundering a garment even if it's been worn *just once.*

And even though I wouldn't be a regular socializer - my most recent night on the town in Dublin may have been pre-Millennium - I've come to believe that women dress their men to be seen by other women. In other words, if a man ventures out of an evening in the company of his partner and his outfit is decidedly un-stylish, the experience will leave him pretty much unfazed. Not so for the woman in his life. (Of course, how he ever got past the front door is a separate question.)

For if the man's outfit is so outlandish as to invite comment, the derision will be directed not at him but at the woman who allowed him to appear in public dressed like a carnival act. Worse still, he might be dressed carelessly *and in the wrong designer labels* - in which case the unfortunate couple should just cut their losses and relocate.

On Cape Cod, where my family holidays for a week each summer, I've noticed that there's a standard uniform of the prosperous leisure classes. White or primary color polo shirt accompanied by khaki shorts or trousers. Then, on the feet, well-constructed boat shoes to suggest that a craft of some size lies docked at a nearby marina.

In Ireland, given the dodgy climate, the fashion among the seriously recreational is for trendy all-weather gear, again with a nautical feel, to give the impression of a sailing background. (Personally, I like to convey a sense of familiarity with the open sea by wearing an "emergency flotation device".)

Having read this far, you're probably wondering what tattered scraps of cloth I drape over myself each day. To be honest, I'm lucky if I'm showered and dressed by noon. Unless, of course, I see my reflection in the computer screen as I'm writing.

In that case, I just go back to bed.

Finally, A Social Program
That Pays For Itself

A FEW YEARS AGO, WRITER Barbara Ehrenreich conceived a brilliant idea for a magazine article, which she later adapted into the best-selling book *Nickel and Dimed: On (Not) Getting By in America*.

Ehrenreich's pitch, boiled down to basics, was this: she would take a series of full-time low-wage jobs, in different parts of the US, and then chronicle her efforts to make ends meet. From the meager earnings that resulted from her considerable labors, she would attempt to pay for her housing, transportation, health care, and - oh, I forgot - her food as well.

It was, as you might expect, an uphill struggle.

An unrepentant social democrat at heart, Ehrenreich also hoped to expose the nonsense that was informing public debate about welfare reform at the time - namely, that earning the minimum wage, stuck in a dead end job, somehow puts you on the road to a better life.

"How, in particular," Ehrenreich wonders in the book's introduction, "were the roughly four million women about to be booted into the labor market...going to make it on $6 or $7 an hour?" (The author herself supplies a rather sardonic reply to this economic dilemma. "Maybe I would…detect in myself the bracing psychological effects of getting out of the house, as promised by the wonks who brought us welfare reform.")

As I've discovered, Ehrenreich's idea and her courageous execution of it, are wickedly irreverent - and make for a cracking good read to boot. (It's also a tale to be read and digested by policies makers here in Ireland.)

But I'd like to go her one better, by proposing a radical overhaul of the way worker relations are handled in the marketplace. How about a new social policy based not on welfare reform, but on retail reform?

As I see it, a new army of service economy workers needs to be recruited from the ranks of the privileged and the well-to-do, marching under the inspiring banner of the Retail Volunteer Corps. Or the RVC, for short.

My own plan, like Ms. Ehrenreich's, is simple enough.

Here in Ireland, just as on Cape Cod or up north in New Hampshire, the local economy is dependent on the kindness of strangers – specifically, those folks who through desperation or determination have decided to leave their former lives behind, in Eastern Europe or Central America, so they might staff the gift shops, restaurants, and hotels that the rest of us frequent on our holidays.

Under my RVC scheme, such workers would get a leg up - or, more likely, a chance to find themselves a second or third job to supplement their income. As I see it, anyone with a second home on the Cape, say, or a holiday bungalow in the West of Ireland, and who earns in excess of 100 k (net) per annum, should be required to put in two weeks a year, gratis, behind the counter. Flipping burgers, taking reservations, handling customer complaints. Wherever they're needed, basically.

The people replaced by these RVCers would receive their normal wages - in effect, they'd be enjoying some extra *paid* vacation time - but they'd also be free to work an extra shift or three themselves, or perhaps find temporary employment elsewhere. (Plus, as a bonus, any labor shortages would be eliminated.)

Just as important, though, my program has real character-building potential. After being sniffed and sneered at, jolted and jeered for a month, our well-off RVC recruits will start to see things from the other side. The "bracing psychological effects" Ms. Ehrenreich envisioned for herself will kick in across the board. We'll all think twice before launching into a full frontal assault over an incorrect fast-food order or a hastily-cleaned hotel room.

And of course, the ultimate benefit is that my program costs the taxpayer nothing. It's basically a win-win situation. Low-wage workers get to earn more without relying on government hand-outs, and holiday-makers are still able to enjoy the comfort and ease of their second homes. (In fact, RVCers might appreciate their seaside or lakefront digs even more after an exhausting stretch at the local fish-and-chip shop or fried clam shack.)

It's a good thing Barbara Ehrenreich came up with *Nickel and Dimed* when she did. Because once some policy wonk or glitzy academic hears of the Retail Volunteer Corps, my scheme will get government approval in no time.

And then the trials and tribulations of the working poor will indeed become a thing of the past.

How Does Your Life Rate?

~~~~~~~~~~

IT'S SAID THAT ART HOLDS a mirror up to life.

If that were truly the case, we'd all be having a lot more sex, and our conversations would be wittier and more substantial than they normally are. (For the sake of argument, I'm taking film as my medium of choice here.)

Given a good script to work from and an experienced director to guide us, we'd all become latter-day Cary Grants and Katherine Hepburns. Or, if action heroes are more your thing, Matt Damon or Angelina Jolie might be your preferred role model.

But there's an even more interesting parallel here: if your life had to be graded like any motion picture, how would it rate? Would your daily antics earn you a PG or an R? (Or maybe even an NC-17 for that long deferred weekend away?)

Well, looking back over the past few months of my own life, I've concluded that while the Disney Corporation would probably approve of my lifestyle, they wouldn't want to commit it to film. In that time I've been a decent dad, an okay husband, an adequate son and sibling. As a "career man", in case you're curious, I've been laughably inept. (Cue an early Farrelly brothers gagfest.)

In short, we're not talking big box office here - even if you were to throw in the latest computer-generated special effects to spice up my daily routine.

So the bottom line is this: as the subject of a major film production (or even an amateurish home movie), my life would put you to sleep after five minutes. If the picture even lasted that long.

But to get serious for a moment (PG-13, scenes of chin-rubbing rumination in the extreme), surely I'm not the only person befuddled by the way the ratings system is applied, and mystified as to why it exists in the first place. Do we judge books or paintings in similar fashion?

The last time I looked, for instance, bookstores were divided into sections determined solely by genre, and the titles on offer - say, in the current affairs or thriller sections - didn't carry any kind of industry code designed to warn readers about the content of a particular book. The argument here seems to be: if people are sensible enough to read in our culture, then they're quite able to choose a book without being guided by a crude ratings system.

Likewise, in museums paintings and other artifacts are grouped according to particular artists or periods. I've never approached an exhibit in the MFA in Boston or the National Gallery in Dublin, and been greeted by a sign saying: "To view these pictures you must be over 18 or in the company of a parent or guardian." As with bookstores, it's assumed that since you've made the effort to visit a museum, you're somewhat aware of what is on offer.

In the case of films - which are reviewed, discussed and advertised *ad nauseam* - the same degree of awareness should be expected. For instance, no one walks into a movie entitled *Texas Woodchipper Vigilantes* and is still asking: "Gee, I wonder what this is going to be about?"

Of course, up to this point I haven't addressed the age-old dilemma which the movie ratings system was drawn up to tackle in the first place - namely, the protection of young minds from unsuitable or excessive material. Expressed on a practical level, the problem becomes: exactly what should we permit our youngsters and adolescents to see when they head out to a movie or, increasingly, when they sit down to play a video game? And is the current industry-based ratings system the best we can come up with to guide them?

(It's a shame the same kind of direction seems to be a one-way street where reading is concerned. When it comes to books, adult authorities seem more concerned with pulling "inappropriate" texts out of kids' hands than suggesting powerful and entertaining stories that will draw them into a lifetime of reading. But that's a topic for another day.)

What, then, is my alternative to the current Hollywood ratings system? Sorry, folks, I don't have one. I'd only ask that we don't overreact (or indeed *under*react) when we start grumbling about the effect on young minds of today's coarser movie productions.

Finally, in talking with our kids about film standards, we might suggest to them that Tinsel Town's focus group-addicted studio heads aren't exactly the hippest people on the planet. And we might build on the discussion by asking them: if your own life were a movie, how would it rate?

Reaching The Simple Life
In A Second Car

～～～～～

BACK IN HIGH SCHOOL, MY literary heroes were Mark Twain and Henry Thoreau. I admired Twain for his irreverent wit and satirical genius, and he remains an influence to this day. In Thoreau I detected a kind of moral resolve that appealed to my adolescent mind - and indeed still does, distinguished as it is by an iconoclastic streak that one rarely encounters these days.

As the years advance, however, and life's steady demands pile up, I've had to pull back from a full embrace of Thoreau's central doctrine, best summed up in his clarion call to "Simplify!, simplify!".

Thoreau's writings came to mind recently after my wife and I had visited a local car dealer. We were interested in buying a new vehicle, intending to trade in our old one. We got the VIP treatment, took our preferred model for a test drive, and sat down with the saleswoman to talk figures.

As it happened, we didn't finalize a deal on the day, but by the time we got home, one thing was certain: we were determined to keep our old car.

So much for Simplify, simplify.

But wait. Sometimes simplifying one's life isn't the straightforward proposition it first appears. For instance, in the short time since we've become a two-car family, certain aspects of our life have become a lot more manageable. My wife is a neonatal nurse-manager in a busy Dublin hospital and her shifts can cover any hour of the day or night. As a result, taking public transit isn't always a safe or practical alternative.

Now that we're doubly enabled in the car department, she can arrange her work schedule to suit her own needs (or to help accommodate those of her colleagues). Before our second vehicle appeared, she'd often have to phone home to query me on my schedule - or, more likely, our son's.

I coach a youth baseball team here and help run a local Boy Scout group, and both activities ideally require a car to be at my disposal. On two occasions this past spring, I had to lug a couple of bulky equipment bags onto Dublin's equivalent of the T - an exercise that amused my fellow passengers to no end - and then haul the bats, balls, helmets, and gloves a short distance to our makeshift diamond.

Likewise with my Scouting efforts. Keeping 18 young Beaver Scouts occupied for an hour requires an increasing amount of material to be at hand - basic stuff for games and crafts, as well as a rudimentary First Aid kit. And that doesn't count the mounting volume of paperwork surrounding any child-centered activity these days.

As for improvements on the home front, I'm now able to do the grocery shopping - or offer a lift to an older neighbor - when my wife is at work.

Of course, I still walk whenever possible, and for days at a time our second car might lie neglected in the driveway. So does that make it a shameful extravagance? Or a valuable necessity? Well, like so many things incorporated into a modern lifestyle, a second car is a little bit of both.

At the other extreme, I've never been able to buy into the

no-car argument. I've read about people who choose such a path, invariably professional folks who decide to live in the city within walking distance of a bus stop or train station.

As I see it, though, not owning a car, far from simplifying one's life, just throws up different set of complications.

Yes, there are always taxis to ferry home the weekly shopping, and buses and trains (and rental cars) for the odd family day out. And it is probably cheaper in the long run to cut loose the family car, given the price of gas and insurance and general upkeep.

But isn't there a greater social cost in *not* owning a car? Reflecting on my own experience, for instance, I think it would be difficult for a car-less person to coach a sports team or lead any other volunteer activity. The personal logistics would simply be unmanageable, at least where scheduling and equipment provision were concerned. In the end, you'd need to have the regular involvement of one or two other people who did have a car.

A similar situation arises when your child receives the inevitable invitation to a classmate's birthday party. Your auto-free state prevents you from ever participating in a carpool to such an event, but good manners dictate that you can't accept rides forever from other parents. The result is that your supposedly self-reliant no-car lifestyle soon starts to look a little naïve.

So how have I reconciled myself to belonging to a two-car family? Well, as I recall, even Henry Thoreau needed a lift from his friends every now and again. And if he were alive today, I'd be able to oblige him.

Awe Just Ain't What It
Used To Be

WHETHER IT'S THE LATEST INSTALLMENT of the Apple iPhone or Microsoft's ever-evolving Windows program, we're encouraged to gaze in wonder at every technological innovation these days. On top of which, we're asked to regard their tireless promoters as a *sui generis* breed of entrepreneur - but with a mystical bent.

On this side of the water, for instance, Microsoft ran a TV ad that equated its new Vista operating system with such objects of wonderment as the Apollo space program, the demolition of the Berlin Wall, and the soccer majesty of Pele. Likewise, the prospect of a new techno-toy from Apple has many otherwise sensible commentators delirious with anticipation.

But let's hold on a minute here. In the end we are talking about a new type of phone - a device that's been around for a while - and a slightly different set of commands for running your computer. Not exactly quantum leap stuff.

Because the range of gadgets in our lives has overwhelmed us in recent years, we've lost sight of some really astounding stuff, much of it produced within our own families.

Consider this: my grandmother left Ireland for Boston in 1930 aboard a White Star ocean liner that set sail from Queenstown (now Cobh) in County Cork. In many respects, such as the route the ship would take and the conditions on board, her journey was quite similar to that undertaken by hundreds of Irish immigrants 18 years earlier on another White Star Liner that also called at Queenstown before setting off for New York. Its name: Titanic.

My grandmother's departure was a common experience in another way. She didn't know if or when she would ever again see the mother and father, sisters and brother she was leaving behind.

In fact, she returned home for the first time in 1953. Her flight from Boston to Shannon Airport on Ireland's west coast took 14 hours and cost $500, which was a fortune at the time, and no doubt involved a degree of danger, discomfort, and uncertainty that is absent from air travel today.

In the intervening 23 years, she'd managed to stay in touch with her parents and siblings by exchanging letters, with maybe the added treat of a very occasional (and extremely expensive) phone call to Ireland.

I'm sure that circumstances very similar to these apply to a lot of American families. So you can see why the tweaking of a hand-held device or the upgrading of a computer system doesn't really get me too excited. And probably wouldn't have done much for people of my grandmother's generation. In their time they'd witnessed the electrification of ordinary households, a general uptake of the automobile, and the emergence of global air travel - not to mention mankind's first serious forays into outer space.

These developments, I reckon, have had far more significant effects on the way we view our lives than anything the R&D folks at Apple or Microsoft can conjure up.

But I'm no Luddite looking to return to an era of simple pleasures and basic conveniences. Far from it. Without the facility of e-mail, my freelance work would take a week or more to reach various outlets around Boston. And though I said I'd continue to write in longhand even after I bought my first laptop, I can't see myself returning to pen and paper anytime soon.

Plus, by living in Ireland, I've pretty much determined that my family and I will have to step on to a plane or a ferry in order to travel. Both these forms of transport, so far as I know, rely on sophisticated piloting systems.

All I'm advocating is a bit of perspective. And skepticism. Steve Jobs at Apple and now Steve Ballmer at Microsoft are treated at times like secular prophets, visionaries who can see things that are out of sight of the rest of us.

When I watch them address a crowd - whether they're rallying the troops at a company conference or unveiling a new product - I'm reminded of *Elmer Gantry* or *The Music Man*. The pomp and circumstance surrounding these corporate revival meetings is impressive. And I don't doubt that their message is sincere and often well-meaning. But it isn't The Way. Computer technology, no matter how sophisticated, won't save us from our own folly or delusions. To accomplish that, we'll really need to start thinking outside the box.

So in the run-up to St. Patrick's Day this year, forget trying to organize all your pub outings on that fancy Blackberry you bought just for the occasion. Instead, after everyone has been alerted - via text message, e-mail, or old-fashioned word of mouth - celebrate the countless immigrant journeys that make the day a truly remarkable occasion.

Has Al Gore Signaled The End Of The Road For Travel Lit?

~~~~~~~~~

In 1975, I was a Medford High School sophomore when I discovered the travel writing of a fellow alumnus, Class of '59's Paul Theroux. His train excursions to Asia and the Far East in *The Great Railway Bazaar*, followed by a similar odyssey through the Americas in *The Old Patagonian Express*, provided a welcome tonic to the required texts few of us had the experience or insight to appreciate back then.

Though I've never acknowledged the debt, Theroux gave me the encouragement to follow a similar path - however haltingly I may have proceeded at times - and he instilled in me a lasting appreciation of modern travel writing and its many fine practitioners, such as Jonathan Raban, Dervla Murphy, and Theroux himself.

But lately I've been wondering whether Al Gore has signaled the end of the road for travel writing as we have known it. Will the long-haul literary excursion become an indefensible extravagance in the face of global warming and the accompanying public outcry that we all need to do our bit to help reduce our "carbon footprint"?

Of course, there will always be exceptions. For instance, Bill Bryson's Appalachian adventure *A Walk in the Woods* relies on an acceptable mode of transport - his own two feet – as does Jack Hitt's entertaining *Off the Road*, which recounts the author's 500-mile trek along the pilgrim's route from central France to Santiago de Compostela in Spain.

And we'll always have the carbon-neutral travel journals of old - whether it's William Bulfin's 1907 Irish bicycle epic *Rambles in Eirinn* or Henry Thoreau's account of his walking tour of Cape Cod, published posthumously in 1865.

But what worries me is that in future we'll miss out on many delightful and informative books like David Lamb's *Stolen Season: A Journey Through America and Baseball's Minor Leagues*. Eco-worriers may wince, but the fact is that *Stolen Season* would not have been written if the author hadn't called into service a 20-foot-long reconditioned recreational vehicle with a very dodgy miles-per-gallon ratio. (The durable RV doubled as home and office during the five months Lamb traveled around minor league America.)

Taking his cue from those classic travel writers who let us know straightaway why they're hitting the road, Lamb informs us that his book is a deliberate act of escapism. Back in the 1980s, he was a foreign correspondent for the *Los Angeles Times* based in the Middle East. While sitting out a shelling of his Beirut hotel, he said to a colleague, "If we get out of here, I'm going to find something to write about that's a million miles from Beirut. Like baseball."

Aided in his quest by his reliable motor home - which he christened "Forty-niner" to reflect his age at the time - Lamb remained true to his word, and *Stolen Season* was published in 1991.

For anyone wishing to understand why the game of baseball continues to excite the American literary imagination, this is a must-read book. It's also a great way to visit those parts of the US generally ignored by the big media outlets.

Still, I have to confess that when I picked my hardback copy off the shelf recently, lured by Opening Day at Fenway Park as well as the resumption of my own baseball career in Dublin, I had some misgivings - a measure no doubt of my own creeping cynicism, given the times we live in. Even though I remember enjoying the book when it first appeared, I was half expecting a sickly sweet trip through small-town America, with baseball as a sappy diversion.

Happily, that wasn't the case. Lamb writes with honesty and understanding, and doesn't whitewash any of the colorful characters he meets along the way: minor league players, managers, and owners, as well as their wives, girlfriends and partners. In addition, his own life story, which kicks off in the prologue, makes for compelling reading.

Lamb grew up in Brookline, Massachusetts, and was heartbroken when his beloved hometown team - the Braves, not the Red Sox - pulled up stakes and moved to Milwaukee in the early 1950s. He remained a fan despite the great distance, and at age 15 succeeded in landing himself a column with the *Milwaukee Journal* after confessing his affliction to the paper's sports editor.

It was an experience that would eventually help propel Lamb into his globe-trotting role as *Los Angeles Times* foreign correspondent - and later moonlighting travel writer.

All of which brings me round to my original concern: how do we accommodate carbon-profligate travel writers in this eco-wary age? Well, I may have the answer. Those of us of a more sedentary nature can extend our CO_2 credits to the likes of David Lamb and Paul Theroux and allow them to traverse the globe on our behalf.

It seems a sensible enough plan to me. Because without travel writers, the world would be a lesser place indeed.

Why I'm Closing The Book On Writing Contests

HERE IN THE LAND OF SAINTS and Scholars, it seems everyone has a chance at winning a lucrative literary prize.

Everyone except me, that is. And believe me, I've tried. At last count I'd entered about a dozen short story competitions in the last two years. And I'd have no trouble entering a dozen more, given that every writing group, arts association, and town council seems to be sponsoring some sort of literature festival these days.

As you might expect, this can result in the kind of reverse cash flow familiar to most freelance writers. Namely, there's plenty of checks going out, but hardly any coming in.

At basically 15 euros per story submission on this side of the water and up to $20 a pop in the States, you soon have to develop the skills of a canny bookmaker - I'm working on the Las Vegas model here, not the Bloomsbury one - and establish a reliable set of odds for yourself.

Put more bluntly, you have to set aside all artistic considerations and ask yourself: what realistic chance do I have of bringing home the bacon?

It's become apparent to me at last - light dawns on Marblehead, as my high school English teacher used to say - that my short story writing to date has only served to invigorate various prize funds. The truth is, my money is ending up in other writers' pockets, without so much as a polite thank-you note in reply. This is something I recognized all along, of course, even as I was firing off a check to the Sean O'Faolain Short Story Contest in Cork, or divulging my Visa details on the Glimmer Train website based in Portland, Oregon.

But like any self-deluding creative type, I allowed my ego to whisper sweet blandishments in my ear. *There's no way you can lose! You're the next S.J. Perelman and Garrison Keillor rolled into one!* I told myself. *The judges would be mad not to give you first prize!*

You get the picture. I'm a sucker for flattery, especially when it comes from such an impeccable source.

Well, after many a failed submission, I'm here to tell you that as good as your story might be, it's far more important that you size up the contest judges before you part with any cash.

Case in point: not so long ago, I submitted a satirical sketch to the Davy Byrne Short Story Contest, which was sponsored by a famous Dublin pub in honor of the centenary of Bloomsday, the fictional date - June 16, 1904 - on which James Joyce's masterwork *Ulysses* is set. As you've guessed by now, I didn't win, place, or show. The winning story - "Honey" by Irish writer Anne Enright - netted the lucky author a whopping 20,000 euros in prize money. (You can bump up the real value of the award by another 25 percent, because here in Ireland such artistic earnings come tax-free.)

According to press reports, contest organizers received nearly 1,100 stories, which means that Ms. Enright should invite me - and over a thousand other chumps - out for a drink to celebrate her hefty payday. We supplied a substantial chunk of her prize money after all, and to be honest, we were never a likely threat to her.

It's a sure bet that, on technique alone, only a small percentage of the submitted stories were ever in contention for the prize. And out of those even fewer, I'm sure, appealed to the judging panel, which in this case consisted of American writer Tobias Wolff, Scottish writer A.L. Kennedy, and the Literary Editor of the *Irish Times*, Caroline Walsh.

If I'd done my homework (and ignored the faint echoes of self-praise ringing in my head), I would have conceded, however reluctantly, that my story, "Why I Won't Be A Media Star In The New Millennium", didn't stand a chance. All three judges, from what I know of their work and their tastes, seem indisposed to my preferred literary influences. (Though they'd have to agree that as prophecy, my fiction is first-rate.) In the end, my 10 euro entry fee would have been better spent bankrolling a night of modest merriment in our local pub.

So the lesson here, I guess, is: Author Beware. At least where writing contests are concerned.

As for the frustration and expense I've encountered over the last two years trying to get my first novel into print - now there's a story that any contest judge would find compelling.

My non-prize-winning story appears later in this book, so you, too, can become a literary judge for a day.

Bringing Myself To Book

Is no writer safe?

During a recent leisurely prowl around Dublin's bookshops, I saw them all: Paul Theroux, Anita Shreve, Patricia Cornwell, even Stephen King, as well as the native crop of Roddy Doyle, Nuala O'Faolain, and Maeve Binchy. Every one of them stacked high and deep. In remainder piles.

Such scenes of commercial carnage can have a chastening effect. As an aspiring novelist myself, I often wonder: why bother? If these heavyweights can't shift units at the suggested retail price, what chance do I have? They're accomplished writers with proven sales records, yet at some point in the production process someone misjudged the public's appetite for the best and the brightest in the publishing game.

It's a tricky business, to be sure. With so many other media on offer, books can seem a bit, well, old-fashioned. (Though if you ask me, they're still far better value than a DVD or CD, both as intellectual enhancements and cultural artifacts.)

More tellingly, perhaps, the proper consideration of a good book requires our time and attention - neither of which we seem to possess in any considerable quantity these days.

So if we're too distracted or hassled as a society to indulge in any serious reading, why do I persist in my own efforts to join the club of published novelists?

Two reasons. First, I find it hard to get through a day without crafting at least a page or two of imaginative prose. And second, because in the end, books matter. They hold our past, our present, and our future - despite the dizzying array of new technology that whirs and buzzes and often grinds menacingly around us.

But while books themselves will never die, maybe the old ways of producing and even distributing them will. This conclusion comes from my own experience in trying to get my first novel into print. Having sent out countless submission packages over the past few years that succeeded only in enriching the Irish postal service, I've now determined that I'm going to do the job myself.

I've come close to finding a traditional publisher on two occasions in Ireland. Back in 2000, I received a glowing letter from a small Dublin publisher saying that my satirical novel, *Designing Dev,* had been accepted for their spring catalogue, paperwork to follow, et cetera. I was amazed and delighted. (And a little worried, since I'd submitted only the first few chapters and at that point had written less than half the book.)

Rather ominously, though, my follow-up phone calls and e-mails went unanswered. Four months later another letter arrived, carrying an altogether different message. Having taken "a fresh look" at my partial manuscript, the publisher in question "wasn't sure that the market was strong enough to justify our taking a chance right now". They were withdrawing their offer.

(Fair enough, I thought. Business is business, after all. Still, that didn't stop me from wishing a pox upon their house.)

My second near miss involved another Irish publisher, which was in the process of being gobbled up by Simon and Schuster, so the international implications were tantalizing, to say the least. On this occasion, I sent in the first three chapters, as is the custom, then scrambled to complete the book as one of the company's hired readers kept requesting further chunks of the story to consider.

In the end, with a serviceable first draft in hand, the CEO herself decided that my satirical tale of political skullduggery seemed a more likely candidate for stateside publication first, since the main character is an Irish-American lad from Boston who's recruited to run for the Irish presidency. Despite the CEO's generous comments about the quality of my writing, as well as the company's emerging transatlantic ties, this was not a job they were willing to take on themselves. Another thanks, but no thanks then.

Several years and many more rejection slips later, I'm no less convinced that my book is better than a lot of mainstream fiction already on the market. But I've had my eyes opened in another way.

At its core, book publishing is a commercial enterprise - as my literary crawl through Dublin's bargain-strewn bookshops reminded me - so why shouldn't I regard my untried novel as just another business start-up requiring investment funds and an effective PR campaign?

This is where the rapidly evolving phenomenon of self-publishing (or on-demand publishing) comes into the picture. I'll leave the details to another day, but it is now within the financial reach of any self-respecting writer to bring out his own book himself. Even given the necessary formatting, proofreading, and cover art expenses to give your work that polished look, it's possible to produce a marketable book for a fraction of what it would cost to start up any other type of business.

After the book's been produced, of course, the author's talent for self-promotion becomes the crucial creative ingredient. But aren't all writers required to play that game, from Stephen King to Bill Bryson to Alice Hoffman?

Initially, I regarded my modest publishing successes in the

freelance market as ends in themselves. Not any longer. I see now that it's all about winning over new readers, breaking into new markets, and developing contacts with editors who might carry a review or a feature about my book-length work. In short, I've come to see that I need a business plan, however informal it might be. Surely, no sensible writer could argue with that approach.

In the absence of a traditional relationship with an agent and a publishing house, then, it's up to me to produce the goods *and* market them. Taking a cue from the various recording artists who've shed (or been dropped by) their old labels and chosen to set up on their own, often through Web-based initiatives, more and more writers, I believe, will opt for this approach in future.

So don't be surprised if I pop up someday soon in a bookstore near you promoting my hilarious self-published send-up of contemporary Ireland. As business ventures go, surely book-making is one of the most reputable you can engage in.

In the end, I made the hard-headed business decision that non-fiction is the way to go in the current climate. Hence the collection you now hold in your hands. But I'm not ready to give up just yet on my novel-writing - so watch out.

Frankly, Candor Not Always
The Last Word

~~~~~~~~~

As a freelance writer without a regularly-appearing column or even a blog to my name, I find it difficult sometimes to connect with my readers. Because I'm never sure precisely where or when my work will turn up, I can't address specific current events or name-check newsworthy politicians or celebrities.

In the parlance of the trade, I'm told, my stuff falls into the "evergreen" category.

So sometimes, usually when I'm stuck for an engaging angle or a brilliant enough idea, I'll draw my family into a column - a practice begun several years back when I wrote about a trip I made to Sicily to reconnect with my father's side of the family.

Looking back over my more recent efforts, I see that my young son - and his dual Dublin-Boston identity - have featured principally in nearly a dozen of my essays and provided the background to a handful more. I've dealt with him carefully on each occasion, resulting in an honest and often affectionate portrayal of our relationship. Anyway, I'm hopeful he'll see it that way, and that in future he won't use my own words to construct a Daddy Dearest-type memoir.

Do I have reason to worry? It would seem so. In our 24/7, tell-all media culture, there seems to be no limit to what people will say or write. When discussing important political topics or vital social issues, this is a good thing. We're often too circumspect in those areas, bowing to PC-inspired self-censorship.

But when dealing with the details of individual private lives, we need to exercise a little more discretion, both as suppliers and consumers of this delicate commodity.

Frankly, candor isn't always the last word on the subject.

Of course, maybe I'm just not moving with the times. Maybe public confessions of marital infidelities, addiction problems, and religious conversions - by celebrities and ordinary folks alike, on TV, the Internet, and in print - are indeed good for the soul and provide the first shared steps on the road to redemption.

At the very least, it provides cheap programming - if not news, as some would like us to believe - for the 24-hour cable channels. And there's something else involved. However much we might deny it, we all derive some measure of smug delight from witnessing another person's self-inflicted distress.

This is especially true in the case of ex-New York Governor and former State Attorney General Eliot Spitzer, whose sexual indiscretions have led to his stepping down from office. Of course, Spitzer's admission of improper conduct, like that of most politicians, doesn't really qualify as candor since it didn't come voluntarily. It was only when the press broke the story, pointing out the apparent hypocrisy of a high-level law-enforcer becoming a willing law-breaker, that he came clean. (If Spitzer had been a B-list celebrity or the child of a more successful parent, on the other hand, he would have videotaped his sexual exploits and posted them on the Web for maximum exposure.)

But despite our fascination with such unfortunate cases,

why should we care? Or, more precisely - given that most of us, I believe, are basically well-meaning - what can we possibly do to help? If a person can't see that appearing on *Jerry Springer* or *Big Brother* might not be the wisest move - and indeed might complicate an already difficult life - well, no fund drive or legislative campaign is going to sort out that fundamental problem. It's the momentary fix of fame these folks are after, thinking it will cure all their ills, and in today's insatiable mass media culture that isn't hard to find.

Of course, I'm talking about short-term renown here, not full-time celebrity. The distinction is important. Round-the-clock celebrities live in a different world, a world dependent on a constant stream of all-embracing publicity. And no matter how often we hear famous singers or film stars decrying the media's intrusion into their personal lives, it's a relationship that neither side can afford to damage to any serious degree.

Ordinary people, on the other hand, are a disposable commodity, no matter how sensational their story might be.

Which brings me round to my initial point. Having advocated a policy of less than full disclosure where one's private life is concerned, will I continue to use my family as subjects in my own writing? You bet. I've come to regard my family-based columns as an informal memoir of sorts that my son (and indeed any of his future offspring) might find interesting one day.

Plus, I can take comfort in the fact that much of the best in world literature is based on personal narrative, from Homer's Greek epics down to Anne Tyler's Baltimore novels.

The trick is in the telling.

Why I'm Addicted
To Disaster TV

I'M NOT BY NATURE A morbid person. Nor do I look for gratuitous thrills in my daily life. "Steady as she goes" could very well be my guiding motto.

So why is it that over the past several months I've become addicted to disaster?

I'll take it in dramatic form - say, Steven Spielberg's *Munich*, Paul Greengrass's *United 93*, or maybe even James Cameron's *Titanic* on a wet holiday afternoon. But I prefer shows like *Situation Critical*, *Seconds From Disaster*, and *Air Crash Investigation*, which feature regularly on the National Geographic Channel here.

Even though the outcome is never in doubt - inevitably the plane crashes, the train goes off the rails, the volcano erupts - the forensic reconstruction of these events keeps me riveted to my seat till the catastrophic end.

In recent weeks, for example, I've been enthralled by the extraordinary stories behind several modern-day mishaps: the collapse of the Sampoong Superstore in Seoul in 1995, the crash of the Concorde in Paris in 2000, and the Mont Blanc Tunnel inferno in 1999. I've also been gripped by such old reliables as the San Francisco earthquake and the crash of the Hindenburg.

Now, before you accuse me of crass ghoulishness, let me take the stand for a moment in my own defense. My initial response to contemporary calamities, such as the recent earthquake in China and cyclone in Burma, isn't: *Gosh, wait till the National Geographic Channel gets a hold of these!* I derive no cheap thrills from watching disaster shows, and I certainly have no desire to become either an on-scene bystander or a participant in the type of events they portray.

Okay, maybe I do sometimes experience a vicarious sense of involvement - which is a quite natural response, I would argue, to such detailed re-enactments. (This doesn't occur, by the way, when I'm viewing a Hollywood film or a made-for-TV movie with a similar theme. Often these can trivialize a real-life tragedy by distorting or taking liberties with the emotions and actions of those involved.)

But there's another reason I continue to watch these shows. In the absence of any defining collective struggle in the US over the past 35 to 40 years - concern over climate change has only recently enjoyed a mass appeal - individual fixations such as relationship issues and dietary trends have taken center stage.

With often cringe-inducing consequences.

For instance, the relentless onslaught of reality TV - combined with websites such as YouTube and Face Book - has had the effect of turning us into a worldwide community of exhibitionists and voyeurs. If you're in any doubt, just look at the latest ratings for *Wife Swap, The Bachelor,* or *So You Think You Can Dance.* (Or go on-line any time of the day or night.)

And even though reality TV thrives not on fulfilled ambitions but on thwarted dreams - watch *Big Brother* and *The Apprentice* if you need confirmation - we seem unable to accept that not everyone in life is a winner, and that modest expectations aren't always a bad thing. (Overbearing parents, take note.)

In contrast, what amazes me after every disaster show is the exceptional courage, dignity, and compassion displayed by ordinary people who find themselves caught up in an extreme situation, whether it's a plane hijacking, a ferry sinking, or a bridge collapse. To observe them recall their ordeal, quietly and often without rancor, and to hear them lament the passing of friends and colleagues and acknowledge the unsung heroics of someone who survived but chose to stay out of the limelight - well, it's enough to restore your faith in humanity. Despite what the average reality TV show would lead you to believe.

So I'll make no excuses. The next series of *Seconds From Disaster* and *Air Crash Investigation* can't come to my TV screen quick enough. And if the producers of *Wife Swap* and *The Apprentice* are listening, I might offer them a few simple words of advice: For heaven's sake, would you ever get real!

Dear Parent:
Please Take Note

~~~~~~~~~~

AS FAR AS I CAN tell, there are no how-to manuals on the subject, no weekend seminars you can attend, no instructional DVDs you can check out of the library.

As with so much else in life, the best guide is just old-fashioned experience - though I'd happily buy the book, attend the seminar, or watch the DVD if it helped me form a coping strategy for the interminable notes, newsletters, and fund-raising appeals my son regularly brings home from his south Dublin primary school.

Some days I get the feeling that learning the three R's isn't the reason he's there at all. I'm convinced his real mission is to serve as an apprentice courier, a sort of Mercury-in-waiting whose day isn't complete until another school-related message has found its way into his backpack.

Of course I jest - but only just. In fact, standing in the kitchen in front of our family notice board, I can see that Brian has been a very busy messenger boy of late. Those notes I'm able to read - the board is three or four sheets deep in places - include:

☐ A school sports and vacation schedule running to the end of the academic year
☐ An update on safety concerns about the school's "Walking Bus" initiative - a scheme that encourages younger children to walk together each morning under adult supervision
☐ A reminder about an upcoming Family Quiz Night organized by the PTA
☐ Separate half-page notes - which I plan to relocate to the fridge door and fan out for emphasis - about a school-sponsored clothing drive and cake sale

Not exactly overwhelming stuff, I know, but that's just the tip of an ever expanding iceberg. In addition to all this hard copy, I receive weekly updates via text message from my son's soccer coach about the times of his games and practice sessions, as well as e-mails from his Cub Scout leader alerting us to any future hikes or off-site meetings.

I shouldn't be grumbling, mind you. When I learned that I was going to become a parent, I understood that my future role would be a multi-dimensional one. In the years it would take to rear a child, I would be mentor, teacher, coach, and counselor. It's only recently, though, that my duties and responsibilities as personal secretary to my son have begun to dawn on me. (Better now, I suppose, than when the college applications and financial aid forms start to come along.)

There's another reason I have no right to complain when it comes to the amount of official correspondence my wife and I are expected to handle on our son's behalf. Over the past few years my voluntary pursuits have included coaching a youth baseball team, leading a local Boy Scout Beaver group, and serving on the school PTA. (If you're seeing a pattern here, you're obviously an involved parent yourself. Or maybe just a foolhardy one who hasn't yet learned how to say no.)

Anyway, at times in these positions, I've been complicit in

several rounds of text messaging, e-mailing and old-fashioned ink-on-paper note distribution.

So I can see the situation from both sides. (Consider me a double agent in this well-intentioned struggle to keep parents involved and informed.) I can appreciate the vacant smiles you sometimes get when you try to hand an information sheet to the moms and dads picking up their kids from an organized activity. But I can also sympathize with school officials and sports coaches who try their best to inform parents about upcoming events only to be greeted with genuine astonishment when a child shows up for a game or a field trip without the necessary gear or clothing.

So what has my dual status taught me about the value of all these homeward-bound announcements? Well, for starters I've learned that a lot of paperwork could be eliminated if we cut out just a fraction of our kids' after-school activities and allowed them simply to play together more. (And please, while we're at it, could we outlaw the term "play-date"?)

And second, I've observed that sometimes the most effective way to hand out information is to restrict its availability. The trick here is to leak some essential details - about a meeting or an activity, say - to a few well-chosen recipients. Once word spreads, human nature will run its course, and those not in the loop at the start will soon express an interest in *writing and distributing a note themselves.*

I can't say I've ever used this technique myself. But the next time my printer ink runs dry, I might just give it a go.

Duty-Free? More Like Dutiful Shopping

IF YOU'RE A RECENT VISITOR to Europe and you returned to the States through one of the Continent's international airports, chances are the following scenario is remarkably familiar:

After maybe ten days of buses, trains, and planes, you've endured a hectic finale to your Old World tour, gathering up memories and mementos at every castle and cathedral along the way. By the time you arrive, exhausted but elated, at the airport check-in desk, you're looking forward to an uneventful - and inexpensive - return home. (The falling dollar has made your visit an even more costly venture than you'd imagined.)

But as soon as you've cleared security, you discover that your vacation budget, already in tatters, is liable to take a further hit. You may have thought you'd left the shops and tourist stalls behind you, but no. If you have a single unspent euro or neglected dollar to your name, some shameless airport retailer wants it. And will likely get it.

Welcome to the world of Duty-Free Shopping.

Of course, as anyone who's been to the Emerald Isle knows, Ireland boasts a couple of exceptional duty-free outlets of its own at Dublin Airport in the east and Shannon Airport in the west. It's only fitting, since the idea of offering a retail experience free from national tariffs and taxes originated here.

In 1951, a forward-thinking civil servant named Brendan O'Regan started the air travel cash registers humming when he opened the world's first duty-free liquor shop at Shannon Airport. (Given the supposed health benefits of a good smoke back then, cigarettes were also offered for sale.)

Initially, only airline stewards were allowed to buy the cheap booze and smokes, as well as a selection of souvenirs and gifts, which they then re-sold to passengers when the plane was in the air.

Later, passengers were allowed to make direct purchases at tax-free prices, though at the start Shannon "Duty-Free" applied only to liquor and tobacco. (Indeed, I recall that my Irish-born grandmother availed of the service in the 1960s and 70s, after summertime visits with her brother and sisters in Cork. She'd return to Boston with the occasional bottle of Bailey's Irish Cream in her possession - as well as several reels of priceless home movies.)

Irish airport officials soon realized, however, that despite the age-old popularity of alcohol and cigarettes, it might be wise to broaden their range of goods. As a result, once you get through security at Dublin or Shannon Airports these days, you step into a virtual department store offering electrical goods, clothing, glassware, cosmetics, and souvenirs - as well as the old reliables.

(Irish-American businessman and philanthropist Charles Feeney also saw the huge potential in duty-free sales. He co-founded Duty Free Shoppers Group in 1960, and today the company is the largest player in the $20 billion global duty-free market.)

Quite clearly, "Offer it and they will buy it" appears to be the mantra where duty-free goods and returning world travelers are concerned. But a more compelling question is: after seeing

Paris or London, Tokyo or New Delhi, why does anyone give a second look to the airport equivalent of a suburban mall?

Being a careful consumer isn't a factor. Given the cut-throat nature of global trade these days, duty-free and "real-world" prices are comparable on many items.

This leaves a more plausible explanation: duty-free shopping exists primarily to exploit the guilt of returning air passengers who somehow slipped up in the gift and souvenir line. They might be business travelers who (almost) forgot about their significant other, or student backpackers who promised their subsidizing parents something special from their travels but couldn't carry it with them along the way.

Either way, guilt - combined with plain good manners - can overcome even the most resolute of travelers.

I fly from Dublin to Boston about twice a year. Even on those visits home when I am absolutely sure that every contingency has been covered, I can't resist picking up an extra Irish calendar or picture book, or maybe a piece of decorative glass or a set of coasters, as I proceed toward my boarding gate. Just in case.

And there are thousands more anxious travelers just like me, all of us contributing in our own small way to the continuous success of duty-free shopping.

According to the on-line literature, duty-free founder Brendan O'Regan was awarded two doctorates of law during his long and distinguished career. What he really deserved, as far as I'm concerned, is a PhD in Consumer Psychology.

Out For A Laugh

O, Danny Boy,
Your Agent's Calling
A Speculative Tale

~~~~~~~~~

EVERY GENERATION OR SO, AN athlete appears who changes the face of a particular sport. In years past, it's been Michael Jordan in basketball, Billie Jean King in tennis, Pele in soccer, and Jackie Robinson (quite literally) in baseball.

Given these athletic forerunners, some visionary scribe should have seen the coming of Boston-based Irishman Danny Flaherty, the man who stood an august sporting body - his native Gaelic Athletic Association - on its amateur ear.

Likewise, it can be stated with unassailable certainty that when Gaelic aficionados convene at their next World Congress in San Diego and hand down their verdict on the most influential player ever to swing a hurley or kick a football, Danny Flaherty will eclipse all his rivals.

For the indisputable fact remains that it was young "Danny Boy" Flaherty (as alert commentators soon dubbed him) who introduced the GAA and its reluctant masters to 100,000 euro "courtesy" contracts for its star players; to the lucrative marketing of county jerseys, caps, and sweatshirts, in Ireland and abroad;

and, most importantly, to the American TV networks and their insatiable appetite for sport.

And, remarkably, he did it all quite by chance …

* * * * * * * * * *

Like many a lad after him, Danny Flaherty learned his native game of hurling in a well-subscribed Sunday morning league in Boston, far from the rolling pitches of his home place outside Rathdrum in County Wicklow.

Of course, Danny didn't invite comparisons with Christy Ring straightaway. (He had never given the Gaelic code the attention it demanded during his schooldays and the deficit showed.) In his early days in Boston, Danny had taken to baseball on TV, then softball in the flesh, spending lazy summer evenings swinging a bat and sipping beer with friends whose athletic yearnings easily outpaced their on-field abilities.

After cowering in his apartment for his first two bone-cracking New England winters, he emerged from hibernation after his third Christmas away, and even bought a pair of second-hand ice skates. Then, for a laugh really, he joined an employee hockey league organized by the staff at "Chez-Paddy's", the French restaurant/Irish bar where he waited tables and pulled pints (some weeks as "Jean-Pierre", others as "Sean Og"). For two hours each week at a neighborhood rink, Danny and his workmates endeavored to remain in an upright position and not inflict grievous bodily harm upon one another. It was all great craic.

But such games were momentary diversions, an insincere expression of a young man's considerable athletic talents. Danny Flaherty understood the moment he picked up a hurley (and asked his friend and future agent, Vic Fleming, how to grip it) that the rush he felt would make him put all other games aside. In fact, as Danny would later say in his ghost-written autobiography, *Boy Wanderer*: "It felt like a miraculous epiphany, an opening up of the world and all its glorious possibilities." Or words to that effect.

Of course, that was before the grueling training sessions, the broken bones and bruised ego, the down-and-dirty legal wrangling over the unauthorized use of his name and image in a Budweiser ad. (He told reporters he was a "7-Up" man, and sales soared.)

After six months of solid practice, Danny was struck by another revelation - namely, that he was toiling in obscurity and earning nothing but rebuke (along with expert instruction) for his long hours of diligent attention to the game. His coaches - a collection of ex-pat GAA devotees who sensed their protégé's worth - told him to forget that he had ever heard of Tiger Woods or Kobe Bryant and their respective riches. His heroes were now distant and anonymous, sporting champions on any given Sunday in Cork or Kilkenny, but perhaps school teachers, bank managers, or computer technicians during the week.

Danny Flaherty was an ad man's dream - six feet four inches tall, 220 pounds (each one distributed for maximum cosmetic effect), with more than a seductive trace of Ireland in his voice - and this advice did not quite square with his understanding of life in America.

In retrospect, it's easy to see why 24-year-old Irishman "Danny Boy" Flaherty might have considered himself an up-and-coming commodity. But he could never have envisioned that his value was set to soar thanks to an unforeseen thunderstorm in Texas that disrupted a nationally-televised baseball game.

During the consequent rain delay, as every sports fan now knows, ESPN erroneously broadcast a showing of the 1990 All-Ireland Hurling Final, thinking it was treating its viewers to an encore presentation of *Hookin' Up With The 'Hood*, a well-received fishing show aimed at inner-city gang members.

Before ESPN executives even had a chance to learn the game's peculiar nomenclature, they were dealing with an unqualified hit on their hands. That night, once play had resumed in Texas, the network's switchboards lit up with calls, 99% of them demanding to see more of that "exuberant whirlwind of timber and limb and leather that the Irish call hurling". (Bob Boozer, *Boston Beacon* TV Sports Critic.)

Tug Fellows, programming chief with ESPN, decided to run with the idea before all this new-found fervor dissipated, as it had, seemingly overnight, for his predecessor's dubious series on the intellectual prowess of professional weightlifters, *They Ain't No Dumb-bells!*.

But rather than dispatch an R&D team to Ireland - "too costly and time-consuming" - Fellows made plans to unearth the same treasure in his own backyard. The next day he jumped behind the wheel of his company-leased Ford Bronco and headed for Boston, less than three hours away from ESPN headquarters in Connecticut. (New York's Irish community was closer, but Fellows preferred the snugger confines of Boston's ethnic neighborhoods.) He conducted an early afternoon inspection of the Hub's better-known Irish pubs and eventually found himself in Brighton, just a few blocks from Danny Flaherty's apartment, as it turned out.

Call it luck or coincidence, but in talking with various bartenders about this new game and its TV potential in the States, Tug Fellows heard one name mentioned more often than any other: Danny Flaherty.

* * * * * * * * * *

(Interlude: The roar of an All-Ireland crowd in Croke Park on a September Sunday, with distinctive shouts of abuse and encouragement rising above the din...)

Nobody thought it would ever happen - the first Super Bowl of Hurling, as it was billed, complete with the Goodyear Blimp flying overhead - but American television is a powerful persuader.

Long-time GAA supporters were unsure how to react when

Danny Flaherty led his team of Major League Hurling All-Stars onto the field at Croke Park that day to vie for the first truly supreme title in hurling against the Kilkenny Cats. The standard of hurling in America had improved considerably since Flaherty's media-fuelled emergence, but Major League Hurling and its proponents were regarded by the worthy brethren back home as just another bunch of well-meaning (and opportunistic) hacks.

The facts tell a different story, however.

Happily-exiled carpenters, plumbers, electricians, and laborers who presumed they had dropped their hurleys forever, were now clutching them with a spirit and enthusiasm unknown even in their youth. Weekend leagues flourished, and major US sporting goods companies were producing thousands of hurleys and sliotars, hand guards and helmets, for the domestic market. One manufacturer went so far as to persuade league-leading Boston to try out its new fiberglass "Hurl-Master" during a match with lowly Long Island. The experiment failed miserably.

In the end, as a visit to the GAA Museum will confirm, the stateside mavericks carried the day courtesy of a pulsating comeback, with Danny Flaherty himself sending over several critical points in the final quarter-hour to silence his critics. Of course, you'd need to triple Croke Park's capacity to accommodate all those who now claim to have been at the game.

Tug Fellows - by now Major League Hurling's first Commissioner - was certainly there, high-fiving his companions in ESPN's Corporate Luxury Box. "We thought we had the talent to beat these guys, but you can never be sure," he told reporters later.

Danny Flaherty's pre-match comments were more decisive, bringing to mind Joe Namath's rousing words before he led his lightly-regarded New York Jets into battle on the gridiron in Super Bowl III.

"We will win, without doubt," Flaherty had predicted. "You can bet the farm on that. And after we win, you know where I'll be going: Disney World!" (Flaherty had decided to get his plug in early, in the event he had a sub-par game and missed out on MVP honors and the attendant perks. No such luck for the GAA.)

The American press corps was mildly amused, recognizing the historical precedent. Irish reporters, especially the older ones steeped in GAA lore and custom, took Flaherty's remarks as a declaration of war, unaccustomed as they were to the hubris that can sometimes overtake a talented young athlete.

Danny Flaherty and his ex-pat teammates toured Ireland for a week with the newly-minted Celtic Cup, applauded by modest crowds at polite receptions wherever they appeared. (It was difficult indeed in those early days for people to accept that an essentially Irish trophy could be leaving the country out of Shannon.) Meanwhile, awaiting the freshly-crowned champions back in the States was an unprecedented honor: an afternoon barbecue and an evening's charades with President Leslie Sternwood and the extended First Family.

In an election year no less, Danny Flaherty, hurling's first international poster boy, was bringing another world championship home to America.

* * * * * * * * * *

Faced with this challenge from afar, a dazed GAA soon blossomed with a fresh vitality, and the organization's treasury (nicely lined by now with American television money) was finally opened to its own players, thanks to the successful worldwide marketing of its product line. The children and grandchildren of Irish emigrants in the United States, Canada, and Australia, it seems, can't get enough of the jerseys, sweatshirts, and equipment on sale in specially-licensed GAA shops from Chicago to Melbourne. (That's why GAA President

Bert Staples was delighted to give away 120,000 euros per annum to Galway footballer and teen heart-throb, Elvis Tierney.)

As for the *agent provocateur* himself, "Danny Boy" Flaherty: after his playing days in Boston and then Seattle were over, he retired contented to a minor celebrity in Wicklow, autographing the odd hurley or sliotar for anyone old enough to recognize him (as well as putting his name to a 450 euros-per-week "Training Academy" for promising junior hurlers).

But one regret never left him. "After we'd won that first championship game and climbed up the Hogan Stand to receive the Cup," Flaherty often said, with a wry smile, "I looked around and kicked myself that I hadn't got a piece of the refurbishment gig at Old Croker."

Transcendental Romance:
The Untold Loves Of
Henry David Thoreau

~~~~~~

THERE IS NO GREATER OUTDOORSMAN in the history of American letters than Henry David Thoreau.

From his many classic works we know much about the man. He lived alone in a drafty shack of his own construction beside Walden Pond in Concord. He hiked deep into the Maine woods to enjoy the singular pleasure of swatting away bugs unknown around Boston. And he spent many an hour on the Cape Cod dunes emptying sand from his shoes.

While his writings may have inspired the likes of Mahatma Gandhi and Martin Luther King, Thoreau was, plain and simple, a wilderness man.

But was he always so keen on exploring New England's uncharted backwaters? And did he always prefer to dwell outside the company of men (and women), preaching a strict gospel of civil disobedience and a Spartan lifestyle to anyone who might listen?

Well, as luck would have it, I've chanced upon a couple of his lesser-known essays (such as "Walking Out with My Baby" and "A Week on the Drink") and put together a more engaging portrait of the man.

For instance, in the course of my research I discovered that far from being an ascetic crank taken to lecturing his contemporaries on their moral failings, Thoreau was responsible for setting up the first known dating agency on the North American continent. His outfit, Literary Liaisons, most notably dispatched Nathaniel Hawthorne and Herman Melville on a double date with twin sisters from Salem. The two couples went missing for over a week before Thoreau received word that his writing colleagues had married their dates after a drunken night on the town, and that lawyers on both sides were burning the midnight paraffin to arrange an amicable parting.

Shortly thereafter, Thoreau established a modeling agency that supplied still-life figures to many of the finest art institutes around Boston. This enterprise collapsed, however, when his models unionized under the terse rubric: *Sketch My Ass!*

But this represents only a small sampling of the diverse episodes that distinguished the life of the Concord naturalist and philosopher. For a fuller examination of this unique character, I refer readers to my ground-breaking study, *A Thoreau-ly Naughty Boy*, which was published recently by Verbiage & Sons in a limited edition, as it turned out. In fact, you may need to hire a private detective to find a copy. A few choice extracts follow.

* * * * * * * * * *

In September, 1839, a scant two years out of Harvard College, Henry Thoreau waded shyly into formal Concord society. At a modest soirée hosted by his friends, the Emersons, he met Miss Rita Davenport, a fair lass of eighteen whose charms, it was said, "could recall a full fleet of sailing men from halfway across the Atlantic". Indeed, her intimate knowledge of the seafaring life puzzled Thoreau throughout their time together.

Still, he was mesmerized by her easy grace and her eagerness to neck. Ralph Emerson, ever the watchful matchmaker, noted the blossoming romance in a letter to Thomas Carlyle: "My handyman [Thoreau] has picked himself quite a plum in Miss Rita Davenport, she being as foxy a chick as there is in Concord."

After weeks of quarreling, however, the two lovers parted, each accusing the other of infidelity. Apparently, Thoreau had spied Miss Davenport escorting several nautically-attired men around town, and she had caught him serenading a woodchuck. The break-up devastated young Thoreau, and he swore an oath never to date again. For recreation thereafter, he attended the local Lyceum, feigning interest in the usual humdrum orations on Free Will and Federalism, until one day his roving eye settled on Miss Elisa Lawrence. A shared distaste for bland oratory united the couple, as Thoreau's journal subsequently suggests: "I have never heard a man's ideas but that a woman's figure (va-va-va-voom!) has expressed them more robustly."

Again, according to Emerson, Thoreau had found himself, if not a soulmate, at least a girl who knew how to enjoy herself. Emerson to Carlyle in August, 1840: "Henry, my gardener and lodger, is never home before dawn these days, spending his nights nurturing a new relationship, as it were. His latest beloved is Miss Elisa Lawrence…She is the kind of girl a boy would be delighted to bring home to his mother - if the old dear administered a bordello."

Thoreau himself got the message when, on their third "date", Miss Lawrence submitted an itemized bill for his inspection.

* * * * * * * * * *

In the spring of 1844, several prominent Transcendentalists were implicated in a regional call girl racket, and for a time investigators suspected Thoreau of handling the Massachusetts side of operations. Always a meticulous accountant of his private affairs, Thoreau kept a daily expense sheet that police regarded as the linchpin of their case. For example, from an entry dated April 12, 1844:

Molasses, ... $1 73
Flour, ... 0 88
Lard, ... 0 65
Frilly Undergarments & Perfume, ... 49 72

According to the *Concord Clarion*, May 10, 1844, however, Thoreau was able to concoct a convincing explanation for the fancy underwear and cologne. The lead editorial for that day ran: "Authorities are satisfied that Mr. Henry Thoreau - currently on seaside retreat on Cape Cod - stands cleared of any involvement in the type of activity we hesitate to mention in a family newspaper."

Critic E.J. Bedwedder, in his monumental study, *Literature and Libido*, also supports Thoreau's innocence, albeit indirectly: "Pimping may have been common enough among certain struggling Romantic poets, but in Transcendental New England it was more the practice to sit on the banks of a secluded pond, beneath a brilliant full moon, and watch for skinny-dippers."

At any rate, the experience badly shook Thoreau's faith in the opposite sex. He felt himself betrayed once, twice, and now a third time. After trying unsuccessfully for weeks to resolve the Woman Problem himself, he turned in desperation to Reverend Harland Crotch - Thoreau's only known appeal to the clergy. Reverend Crotch issued the following advice: "Harold [sic], select yourself a woman who is generally insipid - i.e., plain, emotionless, taciturn, neither pleasant nor difficult to look at. You may never be happy, but you will be far from miserable."

Thoreau decided instead to resume his quest for the perfect mate. In January, 1845, he began courting Tess Wannabuss, a Waltham factory girl. Henry and Tess were ideal cultural complements. He unveiled to her the wonders of Hindu scripture; she instructed him in the joys of mud wrestling. They appeared bonded for life. Emerson to Carlyle in March, 1845: "My horsegroom and his girl have become quite an item in our little town. They are oft-times to be seen down by the village pump, reciting psalms to one another whilst rinsing the mud off."

But the inevitable separation occurred on June 4, 1845, when Tess announced her intention to marry Thoreau's chief rival, manure magnate S.E. Hutchinson. "It is time we brought this whole stinking business to a close," Tess declared coldly in her final correspondence with her one-time *paramour.* Thoreau's journal entry for that day reveals the sense of pain and defeat he must have felt: "My pores have imbibed about as much delight as they can take…The 'Concord Casanova' is calling it quits."

On Independence Day, 1845, Henry Thoreau gave up women and retired to Walden Pond.

Taking A Bite Out Of History

IT IS GENERALLY AGREED THAT in most parts of the developed world, snacking has become an established feature of everyday life. And yet, despite growing concerns that our kids and grandkids could resemble decent-sized dirigibles in years to come, no one has compiled a reliable history of snacking.

Sure, nutritionists regularly have their say, and policy-makers like to gather to discuss the topic (as they snack prodigiously at taxpayers' expense).

But where are the hefty tomes? Where's the learned analysis from which we all might draw some valuable lifestyle lessons?

To correct this oversight, I've put together my own study, which I've called *Snacking: A Between Meals Look at Lite Eating*. A few choice morsels follow.

* * * * * * * * * *

Most historians acknowledge that America is the birthplace of the modern snack. But snacking was not always an accepted way of life in the US.

In Puritan New England, for instance, anyone caught taking an extra bit of salted cod or a portion of "gently-spiced chipped potatoes" between meals would be severely ostracized. As punishment, the accused might often be forced to stand for hours in front of a group of his peers, who would be munching on "great bowls of puffy white bursted corn" and mumbling amongst themselves, "Mmm, such a treat befitteth the scoundrel King of England himself!"

Sometimes, as an added rebuke, the communal snack would be extended toward the shamed individual, only to be withdrawn suddenly amidst "general merriment and the slapping of thighs".

Attitudes toward snacking gradually eased, however, and for this the US owes a debt of gratitude to George Washington. During the exceptionally hard winter of 1781-82, he encouraged the colonial soldiers under his command to "graze freely and widely for any sustenance that might not otherwise be available from your regimental stores".

Even after an early spring thaw and the exceptionally bountiful harvest that followed later in the year, Washington turned a blind eye as his men "improvised unique and tasteful delicacies to dampen their ardent hunger at unusual hours".

Ever the entrepreneur, rabble-rouser Sam Adams seized on this emerging trend to promote a line of high-energy seeds and berries, gathered by local urchins and hawked on street corners around Boston. "Sam's Meddlesome Mix" became an overnight success. With each helping, rebellious Bostonians received a leaflet that sent out a clear message to King George: "Nuts to ye and your whole Court!"

For the next century or so, as scores of inns, taverns, and ale houses appeared in the fledgling United States, snacking took a back seat to the more traditional methods of eating. Formal dining flourished - although purveyors of "victuals on the quick" gained a foothold on the western frontier - and home-cooked meals became the mark of a true "American" household.

But the presidency of William Howard Taft (1909-1913)

changed all that. Many Americans soon came to realize that at nearly 300 pounds, their Chief Executive had to be eating outside of hours. In those bygone days, young boys still aspired to grow up - or indeed out - to be President. Taking Taft as their role model, many believed they could eat their way into the job. As a result, snacking went through a glorious Golden Age that saw the invention of Kandy Korn and the toffee apple. But reality intervened with the onset of the Great Depression, when eating of any description became the exclusive privilege of the upper classes.

Franklin Roosevelt attempted to revive public-spirited snacking through various "New Meal" initiatives, such as the Hoover Jam Project, but a certain skepticism remained. Many people still associated quick, on-the-run eating with total economic collapse, and so were hesitant to consume food unnecessarily.

With military victory in Europe and the Far East in 1945, however, a buoyant spirit returned to American eating patterns. Many GIs had developed a healthy appetite for chocolate and Coca-Cola while overseas, and this craving was passed on to their kids and grandkids. Drugstore counters soon became the hangout of choice for teenaged Americans, resulting in the creation of the root beer float and the "Mile-Long" hot dog.

To this day, America leads the way in snacking innovation - our most recent achievement being the nachos smoothie - and perhaps before too long our love for off-peak eating will be reflected in the Taftian girth of some future US President.

The Massachusetts
Healthcare Lottery

~~~~~~~~~

WHEN I'M TALKING WITH FRIENDS here in Ireland about US politics, I like to point out that my home state of Massachusetts isn't like the rest of the country. We're more progressive and innovative, I'm inclined to boast, in our approach to social problems.

So I was heartened to see that Massachusetts lawmakers are attempting to tackle the healthcare dilemma through a bold new plan that makes insurance cover mandatory, whether it's paid by business, government, or individuals.

Likewise, I see that Massachusetts is now considering getting into the gambling business, with Governor Deval Patrick touting the benefits of building a casino in the Bay State.

These two initiatives are fine as they stand, but with a little tweaking Massachusetts has the makings of a revolutionary social program that could be shared with the rest of the country. Here's the way I see it: legislators should use the techniques that have proved so profitable for the Mass. Lottery to streamline the state's healthcare system.

It's easier than you might think.

Every organization that I know of, from your kids' sports teams to their school's PTA, has raised funds at one time or another by conducting a raffle. Raffles, by their nature, are tedious and intrusive, and if you're like me, you'll run a mile in the opposite direction as soon as someone with a book of tickets starts shuffling your way.

Still, it's a sound concept, one that the Lottery has exploited with some clever marketing and fabulous cash prizes. So, that being the case, maybe the Mass. Dept. of Health needs to start thinking outside the box where its own interests are concerned.

This is where my plan comes into the picture. I'm proposing, quite simply, a statewide Healthcare Lottery, with a range of valuable prizes and payoffs.

Using the scratch ticket scenario for starters, I can see Massachusetts healthcare administrators hitting upon a real PR bonanza with a series of games aimed at those people who still find themselves unable, for one reason or another, to access services.

For instance, wouldn't you risk a couple of bucks on a scratch ticket if three walking frames guaranteed you a hip replacement, on the spot and at no charge? Or how about three sets of crooked teeth entitling you (or a nominated loved one) to free, instant orthodontic care?

Of course, the PR possibilities don't end there. Here in Ireland, TV shows based on scratch card games are extremely popular. Contestants are welcomed into the studio each week, along with a screaming entourage of friends and family, and they proceed to compete for cash and prizes.

Massachusetts should use the same approach. Can you imagine the excitement that would be generated if the mother of an autistic child suddenly found that spinning a roulette wheel and landing on a lucky number entitled her son to specialized care? Scratch card sales would rocket.

What's more, there'd also be a corresponding winner at

home, so the viewing figures (and resulting ad revenue, split between the state and the TV station) would go through the roof.

Now, I can already hear the nay-sayers voicing their usual objections. "The HMOs will never buy into such a plan," they'll be warning, or "Won't a Health Lottery simply add another layer of bureaucracy to a system that's been top-heavy for years?"

Well, here's the beauty part. The state's dedicated healthcare professionals will receive a tax-free top-up to their annual salary for every lottery winner they look after (though they won't be aware of their patient's special status at the time).

And as for the curse of paperwork that afflicts every nurse and doctor these days, all cases involving Health Lottery winners will be conducted with a handshake and a pat on the back. No consent forms or waivers of liability signed off in triplicate and then forwarded to the hospital's legal department. (Some exceptionally fine print on the reverse of all winning tickets will make this abundantly clear.)

So Governor Patrick, what do you say? Prove me right by being the first chief executive in the US to adopt this progressive and innovative scheme. I've even got a great photo op in mind. The setting is the cardiac ICU in one of Boston's many outstanding hospitals. You'd be the center of attention, of course, earnest but proud, flanked on one side by a Lottery winner who's just received a free coronary bypass, and on the other by a lucky medical professional who's suddenly found herself with a little extra money in her pocket.

Let's face it, with this healthcare system, everyone's a winner. *P.S. Ireland could benefit even more from a Health Lottery. Unfortunately, health officials here believe the status quo - long queues, deferred treatments, and makeshift facilities - is just fine, thank you very much.*

Life In The Breakdown Lane

I'M THINKING OF PUTTING TOGETHER a chilling sociological study entitled "When Machines Fail Us". My paper will document a week in the life of a poor slob whom I'll call Mr. X, but who bears a striking physical resemblance to the present writer.

(So that you'll be able to visualize him, let me just say that Mr. X is about 5' 10", with brown hair and green eyes, and is relatively fit for his age, which cannot be revealed on security grounds. His hobbies include walking, reading, and railing at his fate, which has left him mechanically-disinclined to an almost lethal degree. Mr. X also works from home and so knows the *real* value of a functioning household appliance.)

In the course of my work I will relate how, within a maddeningly brief span, Mr. X has lost the use of a couple of key modern conveniences - namely, his washing machine and DVD player. They recently joined the household casualty list, and his vacuum cleaner is only clinging to life thanks to a prodigious application of duct tape.

(It is also worth noting that with his DVD player gone, Mr. X's cable service has decided to act up, so that he is now able to watch three competing channels on the one screen at the same time. Surprisingly, this has not enhanced his viewing experience.)

But it's not only Mr. X's machines that have let him down. In tandem with these mechanical failures, Mr. X himself is dangerously close to breakdown, prompting his friends and family to debate the question: does the continuous verbal abuse of an inanimate appliance call for outside intervention?

Of course, we all know someone like Mr. X (whom we'll call Mr. Y out of consideration for his privacy). Just as we all know that our daily comfort relies on the sustained well-being of the machines in our lives.

Perhaps the most distressing words any individual of adult years is ever likely to hear will come not from a doctor or a teacher or a clergyman. No, the person most likely to reduce you to an emotional wreck will be wearing greasy, oil-stained coveralls and he'll bring your life to a halt by telling you, in a sympathetic voice: "I'm afraid you were right about those knocking sounds you heard under the hood."

He'll then inquire in a concerned way about your long-term job security, knowing that your car is in need of repairs that even the Pentagon hasn't the budget for. The talk will then turn to gaskets and pistons and valves, with the prospect of "a total engine meltdown" thrown in to complete the picture.

This man, who 24 hours ago was a complete stranger, now commands the most important position in your life. As you shift restlessly in your bed at night, you will mutter his name, which you happen to know because it's stitched onto his clothes.

Such is the influence of the machines in our lives.

Try as we might to preach the gospel of self-sufficiency, it's a doctrine that exists more in the realm of theory than in practice. Unless you're prepared to walk everywhere, wash your clothes by hand, and spend your evenings reading by candlelight, it's perhaps a good idea to become a little more familiar with the machines that buzz, whir, and rev around us. (Before they decide to stage an all-out strike, which would leave most of us to our own devices. And that prospect is scary enough to send sales of DIY manuals shooting through the roof - an eventuality covered in my edition under "House Repairs".)

So the next time you encounter Mr. X (he's out of town till late next week), spare a thought for him. He may look a bit bedraggled because his washing machine still regards the spin cycle as a waste of energy. And if he's bleary-eyed, that's because he and his cable guy can't seem to hook up.

As I say, go easy on him. You could be next. Remember: there but for the grace of a smoothly-running Saab, staggers another poor slob.

Superheroes Are People, Too

THERE IS NO GREATER BONDING experience between a father and a son than going together to a blockbuster film featuring a comic book superhero.

I speak from experience here. On two recent occasions, my son and I have found ourselves seated side by side in a darkened theatre, captivated by the respective adventures of Iron Man and the Incredible Hulk.

But like Dr. Bruce Banner, who transforms into the Hulk whenever someone has the misfortune to annoy him, I've found myself undergoing a certain change of late in my attitude towards superheroes. Gone is the unquestioning awe I used to feel as a boy whenever I opened a Marvel comic book to lap up the latest adventures of Spiderman, Thor, and the Fantastic Four.

Sitting with my son in our local megaplex these days, I'm more inclined to apply the rigorous logic of day-to-day life to the extraordinary exploits of my boyhood heroes.

The sad truth is that no matter what your particular superpower might be - whether you can fly like a rocket or lift a city bus with the tip of your finger - reality inevitably intrudes. The utility bill on your space-age lab and workshop needs to be paid, your fleet of futuristic vehicles requires that extra bit of servicing, and as for maintaining that superhero physique, we're talking some seriously expensive dietary supplements.

So with this theme in mind, I've drawn up a list of concerns that contemporary comic book authors might want to address, to make their tales more accessible to mature readers like me.

In the costume line, for starters, today's superhero needs to think long-term and insist on a sensible pair of shoes. Nothing is more likely to shorten a productive crime-fighting career than chronic back problems brought on by inferior footwear. (Someone like The Flash, for instance, would want to consult directly with the R&D people at Nike and Reebok.)

I've noticed, too, that a lot of modern superheroes and arch-villains like to take their skirmishes into outer space - which is fine if you're prepared. This is where a ready supply of sunscreen with SPF 50 (or better) is a must. I don't care how tough or resilient their skin may be, even superheroes need to protect against premature ageing brought on by continuous exposure to the sun's rays.

And as for the general health of today's crime-fighting elite: no one lives forever, even if you are able to withstand the impact of a runaway locomotive or an energy field in the shape of a hammer that comes crashing down on your head. I don't care who ends up paying for it, but I wouldn't let any of my comic book creations lift a finger until I knew they had comprehensive healthcare coverage.

All it takes is a moment's distraction for an accident to happen. Maybe Green Lantern doesn't get his protective force field up in time and the next thing you know he's being carted off to the local ER with burns and lacerations from an undeflected death ray. As I'd script it, this worst-case scenario would have a happy ending: Green Lantern would be covered and he'd have his insurance information on him, ready to be presented at the hospital reception desk, in a secure back pocket.

And lastly, it's essential that today's superheroes - those

with families, anyway - have access to flexible, affordable, and reliable childcare. They can't be worried about being late to pick up the kids as they're battling some criminal mastermind who wants to use his diabolical intelligence to enslave the entire human race. I mean, what's the point of saving the world if your own children are worse off in the end?

Anyway, those are my suggestions for creating a truly modern superhero. The result might not be as glamorous or inspiring as preceding generations of comic book characters. But really, when trouble strikes, who are you going to call - a guy with super stretchy arms or someone who has their kids' best interests at heart and can work within a budget?

Harry Potter, Take A Hike

I'M A LOUSY TREND-SPOTTER. Months, and sometimes years, can pass before I realize, for instance, that girls who are wearing their pajamas in public aren't sleepwalking, or that an iPod isn't a one-man sensory deprivation chamber.

This is partly due to the solitary life I lead. Every morning I hunker down in front of the computer to record my thoughts for an ever-bemused readership. Then I retreat to our garden shed, settle under a naked light bulb with a good book, and wait to be called for dinner. (After which I retire into my iPod for the evening.)

So I'm the last person you'd want to consult vis-à-vis today's changing social or cultural scene. But on several recent visits to Boston area bookstores, I was startled to discover just how far behind the times I was. As I wandered around in search of a book for my young son, I was amazed at the number of fantasy and wizard-related titles that have flooded the kids' market over the last decade or so.

Sure, I'm familiar with the *Narnia* series and the *Lord of the Rings* trilogy. And yes, I've acquainted myself with England's biggest boy wizard. But it seems that every book for kids these days is obliged, by some cozy publishers' agreement, to feature dragons and fairies and even vampires. (Not to mention a spot of time travel.)

Well, better late than never when it comes to spotting emerging trends. So with the final Harry Potter book due out later this summer, I've decided to sneak a children's character of my own into the market, a young girl of such grace and good humor that comparisons will inevitably be made. (And hopefully dismissed in the lower courts.)

Before the lawyers can get involved, then, here's a brief outline of *The Chronicles of Ka-ching!*, my answer to the greatest publishing phenomenon of the last hundred years.

* * * * * * * * * *

Carrie Potter (no relation, people!) wakes one morning to find her world changed beyond belief. She went to bed a boy - a quite normal boy named Larry, in fact, possessed of no special powers worth mentioning, though sporting a pretty nifty surfer dude birthmark - only to find that she is now a girl. (And as such belongs to a reliable book-buying demographic.)

During the night, it appears, she's been visited by the Greenback Fairies, a band of small, perceptive beings who can spot a buck a mile away. Their message to young Larry (again, no relation), now known as Carrie, is simple: we are giving you great powers that will set you up for life - and then some, so you may want to look into getting yourself a good money manager.

At breakfast, Carrie's parents - whom she now sees as two financially inept Struggles - are trying to come up with lunch money and bus fare for her older brother and sister. (Who, it will emerge in Book Three, *Carrie Potter And The Creditor's Stone*, are actually agents of a local lending institution worried about the ability of Carrie's parents to repay a car loan.)

Sensing the tense family dynamic, Carrie reaches into the front pocket of her new designer jeans, which have also appeared miraculously during the night, and fishes out two crisp fifties.

"Here, take these," she says.

Carrie's awestruck siblings reach over, grab the cash, and look approvingly at the portrait of a president they've never seen on money before.

"Whoa, like where'd these come from, bro? ... I mean, sis."

"Yeah, like are you printing them yourself or something?"

"I'm not sure," Carrie says.

"Well try another pocket, would you?" her father implores her, more interested in her sudden solvency than her sex change.

Carrie's mother favors a more comprehensive approach. "I'm going upstairs to search the rest of your clothes," she says.

Within weeks Carrie becomes the most popular girl in school, and she's put into a special class with kids like herself who also woke one morning possessing the power to produce money out of thin air. But sinister forces lurk in the shadows. These are the notorious Bluebloods, a royal line of money magicians who can also summon cash on demand but need a parent's signature first. An ongoing battle (eventful enough, I'm hoping, to sustain at least six books) is soon joined.

Carrie's skirmishes with the Bluebloods over insider trading and shady corporate accounting practices form the basis of the second installment of my series, *Carrie Potter and the Wall Street Shakedown*.

So look out for *The Chronicles of Ka-ching!* (plus loads of tie-in merchandise) appearing soon at a movie theatre, toy store, and fast food outlet near you.

And who knows, maybe even in a bookstore as well.

Odds Are You'll Love This Book

~~~~~~~~~

IT SEEMS YOU CAN'T LOOK at a newspaper or listen to a news report these days without being told the latest mesmerizing findings from a joint *New York Times*/CBS/Bud Light-sponsored opinion poll. No topic is left unexamined - in numerical terms, anyway. Our sexual preferences, political inclinations, and dietary habits are regularly assigned a percentage figure, and then the pundits are off and racing toward some dubious conclusion about our society as a whole.

Editors and TV news directors love this type of easy reporting, which arrives pre-packaged and ready for mass consumption. But just who are the people who supply us with this journalistic equivalent of fast food?

Well, a new book has hit the shelves that casts some light on the shadowy figures behind the multi-million dollar opinion poll industry. Entitled *Survey This! Playing The Numbers With Johnny Pollster*, the book reveals an insider's knowledge of the game and makes for compelling reading.

But just to be sure that you'd read on, I commissioned a poll indicating that 75 percent of the reading public will indeed love the extract that follows.

* * * * * * * * * *

Let's just say that in this game, you can't be averse to a bit of arm-twisting. Should the situation ever arise.

But that's not Johnny Pollster's style. Like my bosses keep telling me, I've got a gift for getting people to open up to me. One look at my mug and they're ready to talk. So what's my secret?

Basically, I just stand outside a movie theatre or restaurant - the busier, the better - pick out some sap who's looking a little vulnerable, then pop a few questions. Like, *Do you approve of the president's performance? How often do you use public transportation?* Or, *You and your lady friend there, would you say you're happy, mildly contented, or ready to dump one another?*

What it comes down to is, I get paid for being nosy. Can you beat that?

Of course, a lot of your johnny-come-latelies prefer the impersonal approach. They'd rather sit back, pick up a phone, work off a checklist. *Could I have five minutes of your time to answer a few questions?* That kind of thing. With the feet up on the desk.

Meanwhile, the person at the other end just wants to hang up. And usually does. But when you're standing there in front of them, making eye contact, getting to know them, it's harder for them to tell you to get lost. At least that's the way I like to do business.

So how'd I get into this game? Just came to it naturally, I guess. Back in elementary school, during recess, I'd wander around the yard pumping contacts for information. *What's up with the flaky sub in Miss Connolly's class? How come no one likes the new kid just came in from out of town?* Basically anything I might be able to use at a later date.

After a while, I started to get a reputation. Anybody had any questions, it was go see Johnny Pollster down in Old Lady Linford's class. People wanted something I had - information.

And they were willing to pay for it. First in line when it was time to go home, a second carton of milk at lunch, maybe a little extra help with the homework.

You know what I'm saying?

Even the teachers knew I was the go-to guy. If they needed to find out what the buzz in the coatroom was all about, or what the Costello twins had really done with their homework, they came to me. But nothing comes cheap in this world. So I'd say, yeah, I got that information, but it'll cost you.

Of course, that isn't what any teacher wants to hear. So I'd have to stay after school on occasion. Which suited me just fine, because there's no place like a detention room for keeping your ear to the ground. I'd listen, take notes, maybe ask a question or two. But nothing too pushy. No respondent likes to feel he's being squeezed. That's a lesson the younger guys out there today don't always remember.

In junior high and high school, it was more of the same. Except I got organized. I had folders and files on everything and everybody. Who did what, where, and how many times each week. Plus, I pretty much invented the exit poll. I used to stand outside Mr. Flaherty's history class, during a big test, then collar the kids on their way out. *Easy or hard?* I'd ask. Also, *What were the main topics? And how much study time would you be talking for a passing grade?*

Then, in my senior year, word got out around town about my numbers game, and the big boys came calling. After a two-hour sit-down with representatives from the Gallup Family, I was a made man.

But like you probably figured, I'm not the type to take orders. So to this day I get to set the questions and assign the hits. I don't like the look of a subject - he's too shifty maybe and I'm only going to catch grief when I ask about his church-going habits - I can wave bye-bye. Then I just put out the feelers for someone in a similar demographic. Only this time with a smile. But not too chatty.

And that, my friends, plain and simple, is what keeps you alive in this racket.

Recipe Is Simple To Become
A Best-selling Irish Author

A FEW YEARS BACK, AN Australian bloke by the name of Brett De La Mare decided to fly his paraglider on to the forecourt of Buckingham Palace. The stunt, apparently, was meant to arouse interest in the airborne Aussie's unpublished book, *Canine Dawn*, a Tarantino-style "sex, money and adventure" novel set in the Australian Outback.

Such daring feats of self-promotion aren't likely to emerge any time soon on the Irish literary scene. At the rate they're reproducing here, PR people are more likely to be falling from the sky than aspiring writers.

Besides, Irish authors still favor the old familiar ways when it comes to securing a book deal. Just ask the poor sap whose artistic plight is chronicled below.

✷ ✷ ✷ ✷ ✷ ✷ ✷ ✷ ✷ ✷

Day One: Who thought it would ever come to this?

After 15 anonymous rejection slips, 57 unreturned phone calls, and innumerable e-mails lost forever in the ether of cyberspace, I've finally realized there's only one solution: I've decided to go on hunger strike for a book deal. I mean, no form of protest is more Irish than turning down a hot meal, am I right? And what publisher is going to resist such a ready-made publicity coup? (Even if I might be a bit weak for book signings.)

My on-again, off-again partner, Priscilla, is unimpressed by the first draft of *Heaven's Haymaker*, my sprawling modern epic of a champion pugilist turned street preacher. She herself is a published poet (if you count the 4-line ditty dashed off in response to a sandwich spread competition), and she's working on a longer opus called "deadbeat daddio", which contains an alarmingly accurate depiction of my daily routine.

On the strength of her first draft (150 words surrounded by the phone numbers of our local takeaway restaurants, which I jotted down before she'd titled the piece), five publishers have expressed an interest in putting out a collection of her work.

"I'm getting an Indian tonight," she tells me, finding the appropriate number in the upper left corner of "daddio", then adds with a smirk, "Care to join me?"

Day Three: A publisher rang today!...For Priscilla. They haven't heard about my hunger strike, though the woman on the phone does admit I sound a bit edgy. "You're probably hypoglycemic," she advises. I manage to stall her, and even bring up the subject of my own unclaimed work, but she politely points out that *Haymaker* doesn't sound sufficiently commercial for them. "We're really only interested in mainstream women's fiction" – i.e., the sort of prattling whimsy that makes air travel bearable – "or else writing that's so far out it's in." Hence their interest in Priscilla, I imagine.

"Do keep me in mind, in case you ever change direction," I say. There is a dismissive sigh at the other end of the phone, which I pass to Priscilla, who responds with a glare. After a few moments she is positively reveling in whatever news she's been given, bouncing on her toes and jiggling a backside that

Michelangelo himself couldn't have chiseled more expertly. Then she turns away and whispers into the phone, "Yeah, he's that, all right, but I haven't the heart to break it off just yet." God, I could use a pint and a bag of chips.

Day Five: It's official: Priscilla received her contract in today's post. A three-book deal with Palaver Books. For starters, they want her to pad out "deadbeat daddio" into a 500-page contemporary saga featuring loads of tedious chat in crowded wine bars about no-hope relationships, and descriptions of sex so off-putting as to make the monastic life an appealing career option.

A reporter did ring today to ask was I the writer who was refusing to ride public transport in order to highlight falling literacy rates. As usual, he has the story arseways. When I explain the situation to him, he pauses for a moment and says, "Nice try, but you're talking to the wrong guy. Let me connect you to our show biz correspondent."

Leave it to the tabloids to trivialize the arts.

Day Eight: Priscilla packed her bags today, even though it's her place. She's been accepted at Shagwood, that ritzy writers' retreat in the back end of nowhere, the one with the humongous sign on the front gate warning: "Trespassers Will Be Portrayed Unfavourably In All Residents' Work."

I did some calling around myself. A few local restaurants need delivery guys – at least I'll get fed. I've decided to give up on the protest. I'll need all my strength to work on my next book, which can't possibly miss. It's called *Balls Between The Ears: Men and The Way We Think*.

The Erasable Child

~~~~~~~~~~~~~~~~

Press Release and Fact Sheet

From: Pharm Fresh Industries, Geneva, Switzerland & Cork, Ireland
To: All Major Media Outlets
Re: New Drug Development

Pharm Fresh Industries is excited to announce a major new breakthrough in the treatment of childhood behavioral disorders with the development of Brataxin.

Brataxin is designed to eliminate unruly or disruptive outbursts in children aged between three and 12 and is delivered in a bright fruit-flavored tablet. Brataxin tested positively in trials conducted among over 1,250 youngsters from 15 different countries and, in an overwhelming majority of cases, was successful in bringing about a quieter, more adaptable child.

Many parents are "at their wits' end" when it comes to dealing with extreme misbehavior (as well as garden-variety disobedience) on the part of their offspring. Pharm Fresh can now offer these beleaguered moms and dads a helping hand, thanks to the ground-breaking work done in our R&D labs by a dedicated team of specialists.

So what makes Brataxin different from its pharmaceutical rivals? Brataxin doesn't just modify or mask an existing condition. Brataxin goes to the root of the problem and *erases* it, creating in the process a veritable blank slate of a child who is then ready to listen and to learn.

Consider the case of Child 451 – a male, aged seven years, four months – whose mother brought him to our testing center because she could no longer countenance or control his tantrums and fits. Rather than attempt to reverse or alter established patterns of behavior, which is the common practice in cases such as this and often provides only a temporary "overlay" remedy, our medical technicians were able to offer a more effective solution. By the name of Brataxin.

Over a preliminary three-day period, Child 451's behavior was scrupulously observed and recorded, along with his mother's heartbreaking attempts to discipline him, or indeed to interact with him in any meaningful way. Child 451 shouted, he spat, he threw objects and tantrums, often in pursuit of an outcome that interested him only momentarily, i.e., increased TV time, greater availability of a favorite snack food, preferred treatment on family outings, etc. Clearly, even at a quite immature stage of development, Child 451 recognized the benefit of establishing ground rules that privileged him and him alone.

Our medical technicians witnessed the problem first-hand, and they were moved by the emotional devastation it was causing. A mother struggling to do her best, a father incapable of connecting due to pre-existing intimacy issues, and two female siblings looking on and wondering where they fit in. Though innately bright and at times personable, Child 451 was heading towards a lifetime of disappointment and unfulfilled ambitions. And he was taking his family along for the ride.

Enter Brataxin.

Over a further four-week period and with his parents'

consent (see attached waiver form), Child 451 was administered Brataxin in two daily doses, "Berry Blitz" in the morning and "Citrus Supreme" in the afternoon. The results were almost immediate, in the form of a more agreeable and compliant youngster. Past patterns of defiant behavior were eradicated – excised, seemingly overnight, with a minimum of time-consuming (and often judgmental) adult intervention.

As we had hoped, our expectations for Brataxin (and for Child 451) were blissfully realized.

Today, Child 451 is every parent's dream. He's on a regular dosage of Brataxin and is back in the social mainstream, at ease among his peers and wonderfully (if sometimes belatedly) responsive to adult supervision.

His long-suffering mom loves to have him around - he's so quiet she hardly knows he's there! - and his teachers wish every pupil was like 451. From the start of the school day until the time the dismissal bell rings, 451 is a model student, going about his work with a tranquil resolve that was unimaginable just a short time back. In fact, as our public relations team noticed in a follow-up visit, the classroom walls 451 used to bounce off are now adorned with his artwork – it's all buttercups and daisies and birds on the wing.

So the next time your child "acts up", maybe the answer is to bring him down. Gently. With Brataxin. A safe and effective way of getting the most out of your child.

Why I Won't Be A Media Star In The New Millennium

~~~~~~~~~~

Monday, May 16 *Front Page Exclusive!*

JUDGE SAYS CLEAN UP YOUR ACT!

By Eamon Hack
Irish Daily Murmur Correspondent

One-time Environmental Golden Boy and Now Convicted Litter Lout Eugene Taylor emerged from his local south Dublin newsagent's yesterday morning looking like a man who could use a friend.

Taylor, seen here carrying his daily paper (not this one!) and some Greenpeace pamphlets (don't drop them!), declined to speak when approached for comment. Passersby made sure to give him a wide berth.

That's what happens when you don't practice what you preach.

Taylor, best known for his outspoken views on environmental issues, was found guilty in District Court last week of "littering with intent" and can now look forward to a small fine and 15 hours of community service cleaning up his neighbourhood park.

Judge Judith Timmins refused to accept Taylor's argument that the rubbish in question, picked off the ground in O'Connell Street, did not belong to him. The disputed debris amounted to a crumpled King crisps packet as well as an expired Dublin Bus ticket. Taylor's high-powered legal team provided expert testimony from his life partner, Fashion Consultant Rachel Clark, that he was in fact a Tayto Man who went to work on his bike and not public transport.

But Litter Warden and Samaritans Volunteer P.J. Daly swore under oath that Taylor was the offending party. And the judge agreed. "I saw it with my own eyes," Daly testified. "It was no accident. As soon as that last crisp went into his mouth, he threw the empty packet in the gutter. And then his bus ticket for good measure. I had to dodge a taxi and a cement lorry to retrieve them."

In sentencing the Environmental Lobby's Favourite Son, Judge Judy vowed she would keep a close eye on this particular wrongdoer. "Sir," she said, "I'll be conducting surprise inspections of your work, so you're advised to look sharp!"

Well, here at the *Murmur*, we've reached our own verdict. Judge Judy has better ways to be spending her time, so we'll perform those watchdog duties for her.

We promise our readers a week-long vigil.

In the name of justice.

Tuesday, May 17 (Page One, Left Hand Column, Continued to Page 4 with Photo)

NICE WORK IF YOU CAN GET IT!

How long does it take a man to eat his breakfast?

Convicted Litter Lout Eugene Taylor was supposed to begin his court-imposed community service at nine o'clock yesterday morning, but close to noon he could still be seen through the double-glazed windows of his palatial suburban semi-d *sipping coffee and lounging in front of the telly!*

As *Murmur* readers will recall, Taylor incurred the wrath of District Court Judge Judith Timmins last week and was ordered to perform 15 hours of clean-up work in his local park. He continues to protest his innocence.

(Repeated attempts to speak with Taylor over the phone and at the door proved unsuccessful - *even though a female acquaintance gained access for coffee and who knows what else at around one!*)

Finally, at 2:14 pm, Taylor appeared ready for a day's work. He emerged from his front door, black refuse bag and litter clamp in hand, and walked the long mile to St. Michael's Park two blocks away.

Dressed in standard issue blue jeans and a white T-shirt, topped off by dark shades and a battered Earth Day '01 baseball cap, Taylor cut a curious figure among the many walkers and leisure-seekers who frequent the park. Several recognized him - thanks to the prominent coverage afforded his case in the *Murmur* - and some people even lent a hand, popping their own sweets wrappers or melting ice creams into his black sack.

Taylor appeared far from pleased with this community effort, however, and even attempted at one point to hand back a wrapper he'd been given. Luckily, the *Murmur* was on site to remind Taylor of his court-ordered duties. His response was to draw back his litter-picker and make a threatening gesture. *(See photo.)*

After less than half an hour, during which he covered *barely 10 square metres* (according to quantity surveyor Douglas White, hired by the *Murmur*), Taylor exited St. Michael's through a rarely-used side gate and headed for his local pub. He spent almost 90 minutes inside and consumed two pints of lager and a bag of Hunky Dory crisps. The empty packet was subsequently discovered under an adjoining bar stool. Also, the paper he was reading (again not this one!) was found to be missing pages 13 to 20. These later turned up in the branches of a small shrub outside the premises.

The *Murmur* has alerted Judge Timmins to these developments.

Wednesday, May 18 (Page One Teaser beneath Masthead, Featuring a Small, Computer-Enhanced Cameo of a Snarling Taylor)

LITTER LOUT THUMBS NOSE AT JUDGE!
See Page 3

While a cyclone of rubbish swirled around a Southside Dublin park, Convicted Litter Lout Eugene Taylor treated himself to hors d'oeuvres and Chablis at a ritzy charity gala in the Mansion House. *(See photo at left.)*

Tireless eco-worrier Taylor, who has time for everything from Brazilian rain forests to Alaskan seals, spent most of yesterday helping to raise funds for a group called Eco, Ergo Sum - when in fact he should have been on his litter rounds at St. Michael's Park!

"It's a disgrace," said pensioner Nuala Devine as she walked her terrier, Mr. Jiggs, through a shifting mosaic of minerals cans, newsprint, and ice cream wrappers. "This park used to be one of Dublin's jewels. Now it's like an open dump. Something ought to be done."

Do you hear that, Mr. Taylor?

Another visitor to the park, jogger Melvyn Jenkins, complained that there aren't nearly enough staff to oversee such a large amenity as St. Michael's. "I run here every day during my lunch break, and I'd be happy to help out. I'm sure it's no easy job looking after this lovely place."

Certainly not when skivers like Taylor feel free to flout the law!

As of nine o'clock yesterday evening, when the gates of St. Michael's were locked for the night, Eugene Taylor was nowhere to be seen, leaving the bins overflowing and at least two Dubliners heartbroken and disgusted at the state of their beloved park.

And in case Taylor thinks he's getting off lightly, the *Murmur* reached Judge Judith Timmins at her home last night and she has promised to follow up on our report.

Thursday, May 19 (Page 6, Lower Right Corner, Partly Obscured by an Uneven Fold)

JUDGE THREATENS LITTER LOUT WITH JAIL

Judge Judith Timmins sent out a clear message to lawbreakers yesterday: Don't mess with my court!

In an angry showdown outside St. Michael's Park with Eugene Taylor, Judge Judy spared no one's blushes when she told the Convicted Litter Lout to "pick up this park this instant! Or you'll be back in my court, pronto!".

Taylor was leaning against the park's front gate, poking distractedly at the scattered remains of several car ashtrays, when the judge read him the riot act.

Taking the law (and the lawbreaker) into her own hands, Judge Judy marched Taylor into the park and for the remainder of her lunch break supervised his clean-up efforts.

Visitors to this tarnished jewel in Dublin's park system applauded the judge's hands-on approach to sentencing.

"She didn't even bother taking off her wig and gown. Fair

dues to her," said local man Paddy Murray, who a few moments later was seen to snuff out a fag and put the spent butt in his trouser pocket.

"It'd be no harm if more of them stepped down from the bench to check up on cases," said Betty O'Neill, who comes to the park daily. "We could do with more like her. She's a mighty woman. There's not many would do what she done."

With his black bag full and the judge happy with his work, Taylor left the park at about 1:45 pm.

When approached by the *Murmur* for a comment, this normally articulate and erudite spokesman on environmental issues could only mutter, "F*** off, you tossers!"

He'll be up on public order charges next!

Friday, May 20 *Front Page Photo Exclusive!* Wake Up Call!
BACKBENCH TDS CAUGHT SLEEPING ON THE JOB
Is Your Rep One Of The Dozy Dozen?
(Inside, on Page 14, Tucked below an Ad for a Psychic Consultant Who'll Assist in Selecting Your Lottery Numbers)

DONE AND DUSTED!

Environmental Golden Boy Eugene Taylor will restore some lustre to his tarnished reputation when he finishes a court-ordered stint of community service later today.

Taylor has performed some valuable clean-up work in St. Michael's Park during the week, and thanks to a forward-looking judge his efforts serve as an example of what can be achieved in the criminal justice system.

We at the *Murmur* salute Taylor and wish him well in his future endeavours.

Brother, Can You Spare A Crime?

The private eye business is a funny kind of commerce. You can go for weeks without even a suggestion of a job and then Pow!, you find yourself listening to so many offers that your ears start to tingle. In this business it's either feast or famine. And lately, needless to say, it's been more of the latter.

Despite all the talk about government bailouts to ailing industries, I've yet to see a dime myself. Maybe now that the Dems are running D.C., that'll change. All I know is I'm not holding my breath.

Anyway, I was closing up shop early the other day when my cell phone went off. Even though I didn't recognize the number, I pressed "Answer" and clapped the thing to my ear. Before I had a chance to speak, a voice echoed at the other end.

"Hello, can you hear me? Is this Ron Barnstorm - *Things Found While You Wait*?"

I'd used my last few bucks to place an ad in the Yellow Pages.

"Yeah," I said. "You're crystal clear. What can I do for you?"

"The name's Parsley. Sprig Parsley. I'd like you to find something for me - and fast. Are you interested?"

"Sure," I said. "What's your trouble? Blackmailing mistress? Two-timing wife?"

He laughed. "I wish it were that simple. What I have in mind is much tougher." He paused for effect. "I want you to find me a job."

I hadn't seen one myself for some time, so I asked Parsley for a description.

"You'd recognize one quick enough if it were offered to you," he said. "Forty hours a week, guaranteed salary, paid vacation, maybe even a health and pension plan if you're lucky enough to find a boss who still thinks it's the 1950s. Forget about any stimulus packages. The genuine ones are pretty scarce these days unless you're an under-25 polyglot computer geek with a bio-chem and accountancy background. Can you do it?"

"Listen," I said, "you're talking to the guy who found jobs for over a hundred laid-off computer technicians after the dot-com bust in '01. OK, so maybe circus work wasn't their thing. Give me a few days. We'll settle up then."

I wrote down Parsley's address and hung up. This was my first job in months, and the prospects looked pretty bleak. Still, the legwork had to go on.

My strategy was a simple one. First, I'd visit the neighborhood career center, then I'd fill out some job applications at the local mall - assuming they hadn't chained the doors shut.

The career center was busy and the mood tense, but the woman behind the counter brightened when I approached. Her smile intrigued me like the Mona Lisa's, and her eyes and hair were straight out of Rubens - Phil Rubens, the caricature artist.

"Hello," I said. "I'm looking for a job."

"You and a couple hundred others," she said. "I might have something if you're willing to work long hours for peanuts. And by the way," she added, "if you're a reporter, I didn't say that."

"No, you don't understand. The job's not for me. It's for a client. I'm a private detective. In fact, I'm working right now."

"Funny stuff," she said. "Here are a few forms. Work on those for me."

On the applications she gave me, I did my best to portray Parsley in a favorable light, but since I didn't know the guy very well and my fiction-writing skills could use a week or two at Bread Loaf, I wasn't betting on finding a job for him overnight.

My car needed repairs I couldn't afford, so after the career center I walked to the local mall to eyeball any opportunities there. I was ready to give up and go home when I saw a small notice taped to the wall next to a well-known hamburger joint that's fronted by a guy with orange hair and an addiction to floppy shoes and face paint. You know the place. Anyway, the notice read: *Now taking applications for full and part-time positions. Enquire at counter.* I stepped up pronto. Again more form-filling, but this time I was told to come back, in a day or so, when there would almost certainly be an opening, probably on the grill.

My old sleuthing skills were as sharp as ever. Before you could say "Would you like fries with that?", I'd sniffed out a promise of employment from a highly respected restaurateur. I decided to surprise Parsley with the news of my success.

When I arrived at the address he'd given me, I stood back in bewilderment. There was more general pizzazz about the place than you'd expect to see onstage at a Madonna concert. Could this really be the residence of a man desperate for work? My instincts went on high alert.

I pressed the bell. A couple of dames with advanced degrees in pulchritude answered the door.

"Good evening," I said. "Is Mr. Parsley at home?"

The two beauties stepped back like I was a bad smell, then went to fetch the man of the house.

"Barnstorm, I've been trying to reach you all day," Parsley said as he entered the hallway. "I won't be needing your services after all. Turns out I hit Megabucks last night. Found my ticket right after I called you. Three hundred thou per annum for the next 20 years. Can you beat that?"

"Congratulations," I said. "Now if you'll just cover my expenses for the day and top it off with a modest fee, I'll be on my way."

"Expenses? Fee? Didn't you hear me, flatfoot? I don't need you. Butch, Bruno, take our guest for a spin in the new Escalade. But don't mess up the upholstery. In fact, just wrap him up tight and throw him in the trunk." Two behemoths then charged at me with the force of an Apollo rocket. In a second I was in orbit.

I woke up the next morning on a beach somewhere, minus my towel and tanning lotion, and my body felt like a jigsaw puzzle whose pieces didn't quite jibe. When I got back to my office about an hour later, I poured myself a medicinal cocktail.

Then I waited for my cell phone to ring. Like the new guy in the Oval Office keeps telling us, there's nothing bolder than a bit of hope.